Rust Programming language for Network

Build Fast, Secure, and Scalable Systems

Jeff Stuart

3

Discover Other Books in the Series

"Rust Programming Language for Beginners: The Ultimate Beginner's Guide to Safe and Fast Programming"

"Rust Programming Language for Operating Systems: Build Secure and High-Performance Operating Systems in Rust"

"Rust Programming Language for Web Assembly: Build Blazing-Fast, Next-Gen Web Applications"

"Rust Programming Language for Web Development: Building High-Performance Web Applications and APIs"

"Rust Programming Language for Blockchains: Build Secure, Scalable, and High-Performance Distributed Systems"

"Rust Programming Language for Cybersecurity: Writing Secure Code to Implementing Advanced Cryptographic Solutions"

"Rust Programming Language for IoT: The Complete Guide to Developing Secure and Efficient Smart Devices"

"Rust programming Language for Artificial Intelligence: High-performance machine learning with unmatched speed, memory safety, and concurrency from AI innovation"

Disclaimer

The information provided in *"Rust for **Network Programming: Build Fast, Secure, and Scalable Systems"*** by Jeff Stuart is intended solely for educational and informational purposes.

Readers are encouraged to consult qualified professionals or official documentation for specific technical, legal, or professional guidance related to their projects.

Introduction

In a time when the digital environment is advancing at an extraordinary rate, the necessity for robust and efficient networking systems has reached unprecedented levels. As applications grow increasingly intricate and the amount of data transmitted over networks surges, developers encounter distinct challenges in creating systems that are not only swift and scalable but also secure and resilient. This is where Rust, a contemporary programming language that prioritizes safety and performance, becomes relevant.

"**Rust for Network Programming: Build Fast, Secure, and Scalable Systems**" aims to provide developers, engineers, and enthusiasts with the essential knowledge and skills to fully leverage Rust in the realm of network programming. Whether you are an experienced developer seeking to broaden your expertise or a novice eager to explore the domain of high-performance networking, this book will act as your all-encompassing resource.

Why Choose Rust?

Rust distinguishes itself among programming languages due to its exceptional blend of features that are vital for developing networked applications. With a strong focus on memory safety and concurrency without data races, Rust enables developers to produce software that is not only efficient but also devoid of the common vulnerabilities that affect traditional languages. This aspect is especially critical in network programming, where safety and security are of utmost importance. In this book, we will explore how Rust's powerful abstractions and tools enable the creation of systems that can handle high load and scale effortlessly. You will learn how to leverage Rust's ecosystem, including libraries and frameworks tailored for networking, to design applications that are not only reliable and fast, but also maintainable in the face of constant change.

What to Expect

Each chapter will guide you through vital concepts, practical techniques, and real-world examples, focusing on various aspects of network programming using Rust. From building basic TCP/UDP clients and servers to implementing advanced features such as asynchronous programming and error handling, you will gain

hands-on experience that reinforces the principles covered in the text.

Additionally, we'll delve into best practices for security in networked applications, including techniques for mitigating common vulnerabilities such as the risk of buffer overflows and data leaks. By the end of this book, you will not only understand how to write efficient Rust code but also how to secure your applications against potential threats lurking in the network.

Who This Book Is For

This book is intended for a diverse audience, ranging from experienced programmers familiar with network concepts looking to expand their programming languages to newcomers eager to enter the field of network programming. Whether you are developing internal tools or consumer-facing applications, the knowledge gained from this book will be invaluable.

Join the Journey

As we embark on this journey into Rust and network programming, I encourage you to engage with the material, experiment with code, and think critically about the challenges presented. The world of networking is vast and continually changing, but with Rust at your fingertips, you will be well-equipped to tackle any problem that comes your way.

Chapter 1: Getting Started with Rust

Created by Mozilla, Rust is exceptionally advantageous for network programming because of its proficient management of low-level intricacies and its robust type system that aids in mitigating runtime errors. The ownership model inherent in Rust enables developers to construct concurrent applications without the concern of data races, a crucial aspect in network applications where multiple processes may operate concurrently.

In this chapter, we will delve into the fundamental principles of Rust and their application in developing resilient and efficient network programs. We will discuss the process of establishing your development environment, grasping the essentials of Rust syntax, and building your initial straightforward network application.## Setting Up Your Development Environment

Before diving into coding, let's set up your development environment. Follow these steps: ### 1. Install Rust

Rust can be easily installed using `rustup`, a tool for managing Rust versions and associated tools. Open your terminal and run:

```bash
curl --proto '=https' --tlsv1.2 -sSf https://sh.rustup.rs | sh
```

This command will download and install `rustup`. Once installed, you can update your path by adding the following line to your shell configuration file (e.g., `.bashrc`, `.zshrc`):

```bash
export PATH="$HOME/.cargo/bin:$PATH"
```

Restart your terminal or run `source <your_shell_config>` to apply the changes. ### 2. Verify Installation

After the installation is complete, verify that Rust is installed correctly by checking the version:

```bash
rustc --version
```

You should see the version of Rust displayed in the terminal. ### 3. Setting Up a Project

To create a new Rust project, use `cargo`, Rust's package manager and build system. Create a new project by running:

```bash
cargo new rust_network_example cd rust_network_example
```

This command creates a new directory with the necessary files and folder structure to get you started. ## Basic Syntax and Concepts

Before getting into network programming, it's important to understand some basic concepts and syntax in Rust.

Variables and Data Types

In Rust, you can declare variables using the `let` keyword. By default, variables are immutable, meaning you cannot change their value once set. You can make a variable mutable by using the `mut` keyword.

```rust
let x = 5; // immutable

let mut y = 10; // mutable y += 5; // y is now 15
```

Rust has a rich set of data types, including integers, floating-point numbers, booleans, characters, and various collection types like arrays, vectors, and hash maps.

Functions

Functions in Rust are defined using the `fn` keyword, and they require type annotations for parameters and return types.

```rust
fn add(a: i32, b: i32) -> i32 { a + b
}
```

Error Handling

Rust's approach to error handling involves the `Result` and `Option` types. Understanding how to handle errors gracefully is crucial for network programming due to the unpredictable nature of network operations.

```rust
fn    might_fail()    ->    Result<String,    String>    {    if
```

```
    some_condition {
        Ok("Success!".to_string())
    } else {
        Err("Failed!".to_string())
    }
}
```

Creating a Simple TCP Server

Now that you have a grasp of Rust's basic syntax, it's time to dive into network programming. Let's create a simple TCP server that can accept incoming connections and echo back messages.

Step 1: Add Dependencies

Open `Cargo.toml` and add the following dependency for asynchronous programming:

```toml
[dependencies]
tokio = { version = "1", features = ["full"] }
```

`Tokio` is a runtime for writing reliable asynchronous applications with Rust. It provides the essential building blocks required for network programming.

Step 2: Write the Server Code

Now, let's create a TCP server in the `src/main.rs` file:

```rust
```

```rust
use tokio::net::{TcpListener, TcpStream};
use tokio::io::{AsyncBufReadExt, AsyncWriteExt, BufReader};
#[tokio::main] async fn main() {
// Bind the server to local address
let listener = TcpListener::bind("127.0.0.1:8080").await.unwrap();
println!("Server running on 127.0.0.1:8080");
loop {
// Accept incoming connections
let (socket, _) = listener.accept().await.unwrap();
tokio::spawn(async move {

handle_connection(socket).await;

});
}
}
async fn handle_connection(socket: TcpStream) { let mut
reader = BufReader::new(socket);

let mut buf = String::new();
// Read incoming data
while reader.read_line(&mut buf).await.unwrap() > 0 {
// Echo back the received message
reader.get_mut().write_all(buf.as_bytes()).await.unwrap()
; buf.clear(); // Clear buffer for new data
}
```

```
}
```
```

### Step 3: Run the Server

To run your server, simply execute:

```bash cargo run
```

You should see "Server running on 127.0.0.1:8080" in the terminal.

Step 4: Test the Server

You can test your TCP server using `telnet` or any network client. Open another terminal and execute:

```bash

telnet 127.0.0.1 8080
```

Type a message and press enter. You should see the same message echoed back.

We covered how to set up your environment, explored Rust's syntax, and built a simple TCP server. Rust's focus on safety and performance makes it an excellent choice for building reliable network applications.

Setting Up Your Rust Environment

This chapter will guide you through the process of setting
```

up your Rust environment specifically tailored for network programming. By the end, you will have a solid foundation from which to build robust, efficient, and safe network applications.

1. Installing Rust ### 1.1 Rust Toolchain

The first step in setting up your Rust environment is to install the Rust toolchain. Rust's official package manager, Cargo, simplifies the management of Rust packages and dependencies. To get started, visit the [Rust Official Website](https://www.rust-lang.org/tools/install) and follow the installation instructions.

You can install Rust using `rustup`, which manages Rust versions and associated tools seamlessly. Open your terminal and run:

```bash
curl --proto '=https' --tlsv1.2 -sSf https://sh.rustup.rs | sh
```

This command downloads and installs `rustup`. During the installation, it will allow you to customize your installation, but the default settings are recommended.

1.2 Setting Up PATH

After installation, you need to configure your `PATH` environment variable. This enables you to run Rust commands from any terminal session. Run the following command to update your shell configuration:

```bash
source $HOME/.cargo/env
```

You might want to add this line to your shell configuration file (e.g., `.bashrc`, `.zshrc`) for automatic loading in future terminal sessions.

1.3 Verifying the Installation

To verify that Rust and Cargo are installed correctly, you can check their versions:

```bash
rustc --version cargo --version
```

You should see the version numbers of Rust and Cargo printed in the terminal. If you encounter any errors, retrace the installation steps or consult the Rust documentation.

2. Setting Up an Integrated Development Environment (IDE)

While Rust can be developed using any text editor, using an IDE with Rust support can dramatically improve productivity. Popular choices include:

Visual Studio Code: A widely used code editor with Rust plugins available.

IntelliJ IDEA: It offers a robust Rust IDE via the Rust plugin which provides advanced features. ### 2.1 Visual Studio Code Setup

Install Visual Studio Code from the [official website](https://code.visualstudio.com/).

Install Rust Analyzer: Open VS Code, go to the

Extensions view (Ctrl+Shift+X), and search for "Rust Analyzer." Install it for enhanced language support.

Configure Rust Analyzer: You may need to enable cargo workspaces or customize settings through the command palette (Ctrl+Shift+P) by typing 'Rust Analyzer: Workspace`.

2.2 IntelliJ IDEA Setup

Download IntelliJ IDEA from the [JetBrains website](https://www.jetbrains.com/idea/).

Install the Rust Plugin: Once IntelliJ IDEA is installed, go to File > Settings > Plugins, then search for and install the Rust plugin.

Create a New Rust Project: Choose New Project from the welcome screen, select Rust, and follow the prompts.

3. Creating Your First Network Application ### 3.1 Project Setup with Cargo

Now that we have Rust and the IDE ready, let's create a simple network application. Open your terminal and execute the following commands:

```bash
cargo new rust_network_app cd rust_network_app
```

This command will create a new directory called `rust_network_app` with the basic structure of a Rust project.

3.2 Adding Dependencies

For network programming in Rust, you will typically use

libraries that simplify tasks such as HTTP requests or TCP connections. For this example, we will add the `tokio` crate, which is an asynchronous runtime for Rust. Update your `Cargo.toml` file by adding:

```toml
[dependencies]
tokio = { version = "1", features = ["full"] }
```

3.3 Writing a Simple TCP Server

Open the `src/main.rs` file in your project directory and replace its content with the following code for a simple TCP server:

```rust
use tokio::net::TcpListener; use tokio::prelude::*;

#[tokio::main]
async fn main() -> std::io::Result<()> {

let listener = TcpListener::bind("127.0.0.1:8080").await?;
println!("Listening on {}", listener.local_addr()?);

loop {

let (socket, _) = listener.accept().await?;
tokio::spawn(async move {

let buf = vec![0u8; 1024];

let mut reader = tokio::io::BufReader::new(socket); match
reader.read(&mut buf).await {

Ok(n) if n == 0 => return, Ok(n) => {

println!("Received:                          {}",
```
19

```
String::from_utf8_lossy(&buf[..n]));
}
Err(e) => {
eprintln!("Error reading from socket: {}", e);
}
}
});
}
}
```

3.4 Running Your Application

To run your TCP server, return to your terminal and execute:

```bash
cargo run
```

You should see the message indicating the server is listening on `127.0.0.1:8080`. You can test your server by using tools like `telnet` or `netcat` to connect to the server and send messages.

You installed Rust, configured an IDE, and created a simple TCP server using the `tokio` library. As you advance, explore other libraries such as `reqwest` for HTTP requests and `hyper` for HTTP server applications. With Rust's unique attributes combined with a solid networking library, you can develop high- performance network applications with confidence.

Rust Fundamentals for Beginners

Developed by Mozilla Research, Rust was designed to empower developers with the ability to create reliable and efficient software, free from common pitfalls associated with memory management. Its unique features make it a popular choice for both systems-level programming and application development.

This chapter will provide a comprehensive overview of Rust programming fundamentals, covering its syntax, core concepts, and practical examples to equip you with the knowledge needed to start coding in Rust effectively.

1. Setting Up Your Rust Environment

Before diving into Rust coding, it is imperative to set up the environment. Follow these steps to get started: ### Installing Rust

Rustup: The recommended way to install Rust is through `rustup`, a toolchain installer. To install it, open your terminal and run:

```bash
curl --proto '=https' --tlsv1.2 -sSf https://sh.rustup.rs | sh
```

Configuring Your Path: After installation, ensure that your path is configured correctly. You can check if Rust is installed by running:

```bash
rustc --version
```

```
```

Using Cargo

Cargo is Rust's package manager and build system. It simplifies dependency management and project setup.

Creating a New Project:

```bash
cargo new my_project cd my_project
```

Building the Project:

```bash cargo build
```

Running the Project:

```bash cargo run
```

2. Basic Syntax and Data Types ### Hello, Rust!

Let's start with a simple program that prints "Hello, world!" to the console. Create a file named `main.rs`:

```rust
fn main() { println!("Hello, world!");
}
```

To compile and run this program, use:

```bash cargo run
```

Variables and Data Types

Rust is a statically typed language, which means that the types of all variables must be known at compile time. Variables are immutable by default, making Rust's approach to state management safer.

Declaring Variables

Variables can be declared using the `let` keyword. To make a variable mutable, use the `mut` keyword.

```rust
let x = 5; // immutable variable

let mut y = 10; // mutable variable

y += 5; // valid because y is mutable
```

Basic Data Types

Rust provides several built-in data types:
- **Integers**: `i32`, `u32`, `i64`, `u64`
Floating-Point Numbers: `f32`, `f64`
Boolean: `bool`
Characters: `char`
Tuples: Group multiple values
Arrays: Fixed-size arrays ## 3. Control Flow

Conditional Statements

Rust provides standard control flow constructs, such as `if`, `else if`, and `else`.

```rust
```

```
let number = 10;
if number < 5 { println!("Less than 5");
} else if number < 15 { println!("Between 5 and 15");
} else {

println!("15 or more");
}
```

Looping

Rust has several looping mechanisms: `loop`, `while`, and `for`. #### Infinite Loop

```rust
loop {
println!("This will loop forever!"); break; // Exiting the loop
}
```

While Loop

```rust
let mut count = 0; while count < 5 {
println!("Count: {}", count); count += 1;
}
```

For Loop

The `for` loop is commonly used for iterating over ranges.

```rust
for number in 0..5 { println!("Number: {}", number);
}
```

4. Functions

Functions are essential building blocks in Rust. They allow you to encapsulate code for reuse.

```rust
fn greet(name: &str) { println!("Hello, {}!", name);
}
fn main() { greet("Alice");
}
```

Function with Return Values

```rust
fn add(x: i32, y: i32) -> i32 { x + y // Implicit return
}
```

5. Ownership and Borrowing

One of Rust's central features is its ownership model, which enforces memory safety without a garbage collector.

Ownership Rules

Each value in Rust has a variable that's its **owner**.

A value can only have one owner at a time.

When the owner goes out of scope, the value will be dropped. ### Borrowing

To allow multiple parts of your program to access a value without transferring ownership, Rust uses

borrowing.

```rust
fn main() {

let s = String::from("hello");

let len = calculate_length(&s); // Passing a reference
println!("The length of '{}' is {}", s, len);

}

fn calculate_length(s: &String) -> usize { s.len() // Using the reference

}
```

Mutable Borrowing

A mutable reference allows you to change the borrowed data but can only have one mutable reference at a time.

```rust
fn main() {

let mut s = String::from("hello"); change(&mut s); // Mutable reference

}

fn change(s: &mut String) { s.push_str(", world!");
```

```
}
```
` ` `

In this chapter, we covered the fundamental aspects of Rust programming, including setup, basic syntax, control flow, functions, and ownership principles. Understanding these concepts is crucial for utilizing Rust's unique capabilities effectively.

Chapter 2: Core Concepts in Rust

With its rich type system and ownership semantics, Rust provides developers with unprecedented control over system resources without sacrificing safety. This chapter delves into the core concepts that form the foundation of Rust programming. Understanding these principles is essential for harnessing the full potential of the language and crafting robust, efficient software.

2.1 Ownership and Borrowing

One of Rust's most defining features is its ownership model, which ensures memory safety without requiring a garbage collector. In Rust, every value has a single owner, denoted by a variable. The ownership rules can be summarized as follows:

Each value in Rust has a variable that is its *owner*.

A value can only have one owner at a time.

When the owner goes out of scope, the value is dropped and the memory is freed.

These rules eliminate common programming errors, such as dangling pointers and memory leaks. However, ownership introduces a concept called *borrowing*, which allows references to a value without taking ownership. Borrowing can be immutable or mutable:

Immutable Borrowing: When a value is borrowed immutably, multiple references to it can coexist. However, the owner cannot modify the value until all immutable borrows are released.

Mutable Borrowing: A value can have only one mutable reference at a time, and it cannot be borrowed immutably while it is mutably borrowed. This guarantees exclusive access to the value while it is being modified.

Example: Ownership and Borrowing

```rust
fn main() {

let s1 = String::from("Hello"); // s1 owns the String let s2 = &s1; // s2 borrows s1 immutably

println!("{}", s2);    // Output: Hello

let mut s3 = String::from("World");

let s4 = &mut s3;           // s4 borrows s3 mutably
s4.push_str(", Rust!");                // s4 modifies s3
println!("{}", s3);    // Output: World, Rust!

}
```

2.2 The Type System

Rust has a powerful static type system, which helps catch errors during compilation rather than at runtime. Types in Rust can be categorized into several groups:

Scalar Types: These include integers, floating-point numbers, booleans, and characters. Scalar types represent a single value.

Compound Types: These represent a collection of values and include tuples and arrays.

User-defined Types: Rust allows developers to create custom data types using structures (`structs`), enumerations (`enums`), and traits.

Example: Defining a Struct

```rust
struct Circle { radius: f64,
}
impl Circle {
fn area(&self) -> f64 {
std::f64::consts::PI * self.radius * self.radius
}
}
fn main() {
let circle = Circle { radius: 5.0 }; println!("Area of the circle: {}", circle.area());
}
```

2.3 Pattern Matching

Pattern matching is a powerful feature in Rust that allows for complex control flow based on the structure of data. The `match` statement allows you to compare a value against a series of patterns, making it easy to branch logic based on the value's characteristics.

Example: Using Match

```rust
fn describe_number(num: i32) -> &'static str { match num {
```

```rust
        1 => "One",
        2 => "Two",
        3..=10 => "Between three and ten",
        _ => "Greater than ten or negative",
    }
}
fn main() {
    let number = 5;
    println!("Number description: {}", describe_number(number));
}
```

2.4 Error Handling

Error handling in Rust is built around two types: `Result` and `Option`. The `Result` type is used for functions that can return an error, encapsulating either a successful value or an error value. The `Option` type denotes the possibility of absence of a value, encapsulating either `Some(value)` or `None`.

Example: Using Result and Option

```rust
fn divide(num: f64, denom: f64) -> Result<f64, String> {
    if denom == 0.0 {
        Err(String::from("Cannot divide by zero"))
```

```rust
} else {
Ok(num / denom)
}
}
fn main() {
match divide(10.0, 0.0) {
Ok(result) => println!("Result: {}", result), Err(e) =>
println!("Error: {}", e),
}
}
```

2.5 Concurrency

Rust provides powerful abstractions for concurrent programming, making it easier to write safe multi-threaded code. The language's ownership model eliminates common pitfalls in concurrent programming, such as data races. Threads in Rust are created using the `std::thread` module, and shared data can be managed using atomic types or synchronization primitives such as `Arc` (atomic reference counter) and

`Mutex` (mutual exclusion). ### Example: Creating Threads

```rust
use std::thread;
use std::sync::{Arc, Mutex};
fn main() {
```

```
let counter = Arc::new(Mutex::new(0)); let mut handles =
vec![];

for _ in 0..10 {

let counter = Arc::clone(&counter); let handle =
thread::spawn(move || {

let mut num = counter.lock().unwrap();

*num += 1;

});

handles.push(handle);

}

for handle in handles { handle.join().unwrap();

}

println!("Result: {}", *counter.lock().unwrap());

}
```
```

These principles not only empower developers to write
safer and more efficient code but also streamline the
debugging process by catching errors at compile time.

## Ownership, Borrowing, and Lifetimes Explained

These tools allow Rust to manage memory without
requiring a garbage collector, making it both powerful and
efficient. In this chapter, we will explore these concepts in
```

detail, alongside practical examples to illustrate their workings and significance in Rust development.

1. Ownership

Ownership is the foundational principle of Rust's memory management model. Every piece of data in Rust has a single owner: a variable that is responsible for the data's lifecycle. The owner controls the data's access, and when the owner goes out of scope, the memory for the data is automatically freed. This mechanism ensures that there are no dangling pointers or memory leaks, which are common issues in languages that rely on manual memory management.

Here are the rules of ownership in Rust:

Each value in Rust has a variable that's its owner.

A value can only have one owner at a time.

When the owner goes out of scope, the value will be dropped (its memory freed). ### Example of Ownership

```rust
fn main() {

let s = String::from("Hello, Rust!");

// `s` is the owner of the String value

// The string is used here println!("{}", s);

// When `s` goes out of scope, the memory is automatically freed.

}
```

In the example above, the variable `s` owns the `String` value. When the function `main` finishes execution,

`s` is out of scope, and Rust automatically cleans up the allocated memory. ## 2. Borrowing

While ownership provides a straightforward model for managing data, it can lead to restrictions when trying to share data among different parts of a program. To address this, Rust allows borrowing—giving temporary access to data without transferring ownership. Borrowing comes in two flavors: immutable and mutable.

Immutable Borrowing

By default, Rust allows multiple immutable borrows of a value, meaning that you can read the data but not modify it. This is useful when you want to share data without risking changes.

```rust
fn main() {

let s = String::from("Hello, Borrowing!");


let len = calculate_length(&s); // Borrowing `s` as an immutable reference println!("Length of '{}': {}", s, len);

}

fn calculate_length(s: &String) -> usize {

s.len() // We can read the data, but we cannot modify it

}
```

Mutable Borrowing

Conversely, if you want to mutate a value, you can create a mutable reference. However, Rust enforces strict rules: you can have either multiple immutable references *or* one mutable reference at a time. This ensures data safety and prevents race conditions.

```rust
fn main() {
let mut s = String::from("Hello");
change(&mut s); // Mutably borrowing `s` to change it
println!("{}", s);
}
fn change(s: &mut String) {
s.push_str(", World!"); // Modifying the data through a mutable reference
}
```

In this example, when `change` takes a mutable reference to `s`, the owner of the data (the `main` function) cannot create any other references to `s` until the mutable borrow ends.

3. Lifetimes

Lifetimes are a mechanism Rust uses to track how long references are valid. They ensure that data is not accessed after it has been dropped, reinforcing the safety guarantees provided by the ownership model. Lifetimes are especially important when you have functions that take references as parameters or return references.

Basic Lifetime Annotation

Rust can often infer lifetimes automatically, but there are cases where they must be specified. Here's a simple function with lifetime annotations:

```rust
fn longest<'a>(s1: &'a str, s2: &'a str) -> &'a str { if s1.len() > s2.len() {

s1

} else { s2

}

}
```

In this example, `longest` takes two string slices with the same lifetime `'a` and returns a string slice that has the same lifetime. This tells the compiler that the returned reference will remain valid as long as both input references are valid.

Lifetime Elision

To simplify code, Rust has a set of rules known as lifetime elision, which allows you to omit lifetimes in certain cases. The compiler can infer the lifetimes based on the function signature. There are three main rules for elision, which can reduce boilerplate while maintaining clarity.

By ensuring that each piece of data has a single owner and that access is controlled through explicit borrowing mechanisms, Rust prevents many common programming errors related to memory management. Developers are empowered to write high-performance, concurrent systems while avoiding the pitfalls of memory leaks and data races.

Error Handling: Results, Options, and Unwraps

This chapter explores three fundamental types used in error handling in Rust: `Result`, `Option`, and the use of `unwrap`. We will delve into the principles behind these types, their applications, and best practices for error handling in Rust programs.

1. The `Result` Type

The `Result` type is one of the most important constructs in Rust for managing errors. It is defined as:

```rust
enum Result<T, E> { Ok(T),
Err(E),
}
```

The `Result` type can represent either a successful operation (`Ok`) containing a value of type `T`, or an error (`Err`) containing information of type `E`. This construct makes it easy to propagate errors through a system of functions and ensures that the programmer acknowledges potential failure points.

1.1 Creating and Using `Result`

Creating a `Result` type is straightforward. Here's a simple example of a function that reads a file and returns a `Result`:

```rust
use std::fs::File;

use std::io::{self, Read};

fn read_file_contents(path: &str) -> Result<String, io::Error> { let mut file = File::open(path)?;

let mut contents = String::new();
file.read_to_string(&mut contents)?; Ok(contents)

}
```

In this example:

The `?` operator is used to handle errors succinctly. If `File::open` or `read_to_string` fails, the error is returned immediately from `read_file_contents`.

The function returns `Result<String, io::Error>`, meaning it will provide either the contents of the file or an `io::Error`.

1.2 Handling `Result`

To handle `Result` types, the Rust community commonly employs methods such as `match`, `if let`, and higher-order functions like `map`, `and_then`, and `unwrap_or_else`.

Here's how you might handle the `Result` from the `read_file_contents` function:

```rust
fn main() {
    match read_file_contents("example.txt") {
        Ok(contents) => println!("File contents: {}", contents),
        Err(e) => eprintln!("An error occurred: {}", e),
    }
}
```

Using `match` allows for clear and explicit handling of both success and failure cases. ## 2. The `Option` Type

While `Result` is used for operations that can fail, the `Option` type is employed for cases where a value can be absent. The `Option` type is defined as follows:

```rust
enum Option<T> {
    Some(T),
    None,
}
```

An `Option` can either contain a value (`Some`) or indicate the absence of a value (`None`). This is particularly useful in scenarios where a function might not find a value.

2.1 Creating and Using `Option`

Here's an example of a function that searches for an item in a vector and returns an `Option`:

```rust
```

```rust
fn find_item<T: PartialEq>(vec: &[T], item: T) -> Option<usize> { for (index, value) in vec.iter().enumerate() {

if *value == item { return Some(index);

}

}

None

}
```

2.2 Handling `Option`

Handling `Option` values can also be done using `match`, `if let`, or methods like `unwrap_or`, `map`, and

`and_then`. Here's how we can use `find_item`:

```rust
fn main() {

let items = vec![1, 2, 3, 4, 5]; match find_item(&items, 3) {

Some(index) => println!("Item found at index: {}", index),
None => println!("Item not found"),

}

}
```

The `Option` type enhances code safety, reducing the likelihood of null pointer exceptions that plague many other languages.

3. The `unwrap` Method

While handling `Result` and `Option`, developers may sometimes use `unwrap()` to extract values directly. However, caution is advised. The `unwrap()` method will panic if called on `None` or `Err`.

3.1 Using `unwrap` Wisely

```rust
let contents = read_file_contents("example.txt").unwrap(); let index = find_item(&items, 2).unwrap();
```

While using `unwrap()` may lead to concise code, it can also lead to crashes if assumptions about the presence of values are incorrect. Thus, it is recommended to use `unwrap()` sparingly and only in scenarios where the programmer can confidently predict success.

3.2 Alternatives to `unwrap`

For safer alternatives, `unwrap_or`, `unwrap_or_else`, and `expect` can be utilized. For example, `expect()` provides a custom error message that can assist in debugging:

```rust
let contents = read_file_contents("example.txt").expect("Failed to read file");
```

Understanding when and how to use these constructs effectively allows developers to write safer and more reliable code. While `unwrap` can offer a quick way to access values, it is essential to use it judiciously.

Comprehensive error handling not only helps in debugging but also enhances the overall user experience by gracefully handling errors without crashing.

Chapter 3: Networking Basics in Rust

In this chapter, we will explore the basics of networking in Rust programming, focusing on creating networked applications and utilizing Rust's powerful features for handling asynchronous operations and efficient memory management.

Rust provides several libraries for network programming, most notably the `std::net` module for synchronous operations and the `tokio` and `async-std` libraries for asynchronous processing. This chapter will give you a practical introduction to these tools and demonstrate how to implement simple client-server applications.

1. Understanding Sockets

At the core of networking in programming are sockets, which are endpoints for sending and receiving data across a network. A socket can be thought of as an interface for communication between your application and the network stack of the operating system. In Rust, the `std::net` module provides support for TCP and UDP socket communication.

TCP vs. UDP

TCP (Transmission Control Protocol): A connection-oriented protocol that guarantees the delivery of data packets in order. It provides reliability and error-checking mechanisms, making it suitable for applications that require consistent data flow, such as web applications and file transfers.

UDP (User Datagram Protocol): A connectionless protocol that does not guarantee delivery or order of packets. It is faster and has lower latency than TCP, making it suitable for real-time applications such as gaming and live video streaming.

Creating a TCP Socket

Let's start by creating a simple TCP server and client to illustrate how resizing the `std::net` module works. #### 1.1 TCP Server Example

The following example creates a basic TCP server that listens for incoming connections on a specified port and echoes back any data it receives:

```rust
use std::net::{TcpListener, TcpStream, SocketAddr}; use std::io::{Read, Write};

fn handle_client(mut stream: TcpStream) { let mut buffer = [0; 1024];

while match stream.read(&mut buffer) { Ok(size) if size > 0 => {

stream.write(&buffer[0..size]).is_ok()

},

_ => false,

} {}

}

fn main() {

let address = "127.0.0.1:7878".parse::<SocketAddr>().unwrap();     let listener = TcpListener::bind(address).expect("Could not bind");
```

```rust
println!("Server listening on {}", address); for stream in listener.incoming() {
    match stream { Ok(stream) => {
        handle_client(stream); println!("Client connected!");
    },
    Err(err) => {
        eprintln!("Failed to accept connection: {}", err);
    },
    }
    }
}
```

In this example, the server listens on `127.0.0.1:7878`, accepts incoming connections, and processes them in the `handle_client` function, which echoes received data back to the client.

1.2 TCP Client Example

Next, let's create a simple client that connects to our server:

```rust
use std::net::TcpStream; use std::io::{Write, Read};

fn main() {
    let mut stream = TcpStream::connect("127.0.0.1:7878").expect("Could not connect");
```

```
let        message        =        b"Hello,        server!";
stream.write(message).expect("Failed to write to server");

let mut buffer = [0; 1024];

let size = stream.read(&mut buffer).expect("Failed to read
from   server");   println!("Received   from   server:   {}",
String::from_utf8_lossy(&buffer[..size]));

}
```

The client connects to the server, sends a message, and
prints out the response it receives. ## 2. Asynchronous
Networking with Tokio

For applications requiring concurrency, Rust's `tokio`
library offers powerful asynchronous paradigms. With

`tokio`, you can handle many connections simultaneously
without blocking the execution of your program. ###
Setting Up Tokio

To use `tokio`, you need to add it as a dependency in your
`Cargo.toml`:

```toml [dependencies]
tokio = { version = "1", features = ["full"] }
```

Asynchronous Server Example

Here's how to create an asynchronous TCP server using
`tokio`:

```rust
```

```rust
use tokio::net::{TcpListener, TcpStream};

use tokio::io::{self, AsyncReadExt, AsyncWriteExt};

async fn handle_client(mut stream: TcpStream) { let mut
buffer = vec![0; 1024];

while let Ok(size) = stream.read(&mut buffer).await { if
size == 0 {

return; // Connection closed
}

stream.write_all(&buffer[..size]).await.expect("Failed   to
write back");

}
}

#[tokio::main] async fn main() {

let                    listener                    =
TcpListener::bind("127.0.0.1:7878").await.expect("Could
not bind");

println!("Async server listening on 127.0.0.1:7878"); loop {

let (stream, _) = listener.accept().await.expect("Failed to
accept connection"); tokio::spawn(handle_client(stream));

}
}
```

In this example, the server listens for incoming
connections asynchronously and spawns a new task for
each client connection to handle its communication.

Conclusion

48

Networking in Rust can range from straightforward synchronous communication to complex asynchronous programming. Understanding the underlying principles of sockets, TCP/UDP, and how to implement them with both `std::net` and `tokio` provides a solid foundation for building networked applications.

In this chapter, we covered the basics of setting up TCP servers and clients, introduced asynchronous programming with the `tokio` library, and discussed the advantages of non-blocking I/O in developing scalable systems.

Introduction to Networking Concepts

This chapter aims to introduce the foundational concepts of networking as they pertain to Rust programming. ## 1.2 What is Rust?

Rust is a systems programming language that prioritizes safety, concurrency, and performance. It is particularly well-suited for applications that require high levels of reliability and efficiency, such as network services. Rust's powerful type system and strict ownership model prevent many of the common bugs associated with memory management, making it an excellent choice for writing robust networking code.

1.3 Key Networking Concepts ### 1.3.1 Protocols

Protocols are the rules or standards that dictate how data is transmitted across a network. Common networking protocols include:

TCP (Transmission Control Protocol): A connection-oriented protocol that ensures reliable and ordered delivery of data packets.

UDP (User Datagram Protocol): A connectionless protocol that allows for fast transmission of data without guaranteeing delivery, often used in applications where speed is critical, such as video streaming or online gaming.

HTTP/HTTPS (Hypertext Transfer Protocol/Secure): The protocol used for transferring web pages, where HTTPS adds an encryption layer for security.

1.3.2 Sockets

Sockets are endpoints for sending and receiving data across a network. In Rust, the `std::net` module provides a robust framework for working with sockets. Understanding how to implement both TCP and UDP sockets is essential for building effective networked applications.

1.3.3 Client-Server Model

One of the foundational paradigms in networking is the client-server model, wherein the client makes requests for services or resources, and the server responds to those requests. Rust can easily facilitate this model by allowing developers to implement both the client-side and server-side components efficiently.

1.3.4 Asynchronous Programming

In networking applications, particularly those that require high concurrency—like web servers or chat applications—handling multiple connections simultaneously is critical. Rust's asynchronous programming capabilities, powered by the `async`/`await` syntax and libraries like `tokio` or `async-std`, allow developers to write scalable and efficient network applications.

1.4 Setting Up a Rust Networking Environment

Before diving into coding, it's essential to set up a development environment. To get started with networking in Rust, you will need:

Rust Installation: Install Rust through `rustup`, which also sets up `cargo`, Rust's package manager and build system.

Libraries: While the standard library offers significant networking support, you may also want to explore external crates like `tokio` for asynchronous tasks and `reqwest` for handling HTTP requests.

Development Tools: Use an IDE or text editor equipped with Rust plugins for enhanced development experience. Tools like Visual Studio Code or IntelliJ with the Rust plugin can simplify the development process.

1.5 Your First Networking Application

To illustrate the concepts covered in this chapter, let's create a simple TCP server and client in Rust. ### 1.5.1 TCP Server Example

```rust
use std::net::{TcpListener, TcpStream}; use std::io::{Read, Write};

fn handle_client(mut stream: TcpStream) { let mut buffer = [0; 1024];

match stream.read(&mut buffer) { Ok(_) => {

stream.write(&buffer).unwrap(); // Echo back the received message
},
```

```rust
Err(e) => {
eprintln!("Failed to read from socket: {}", e);
},
}
}
fn main() {
let listener = TcpListener::bind("127.0.0.1:7878").unwrap();
println!("Server is running on port 7878.");
for stream in listener.incoming() { match stream {
Ok(stream) => handle_client(stream), Err(e) => {
eprintln!("Failed to accept connection: {}", e);
},
}
}
}
```

1.5.2 TCP Client Example

```rust
use std::net::TcpStream; use std::io::{Write, Read};
fn main() {
let mut stream = TcpStream::connect("127.0.0.1:7878").unwrap(); let
message = b"Hello, server!";
```

```
stream.write(message).unwrap();

let mut buffer = [0; 1024];

let bytes_read = stream.read(&mut buffer).unwrap();

println!("Received:                        {}",
String::from_utf8_lossy(&buffer[..bytes_read]));

}
```
```

We also set the stage for building simple network applications by examining the basics of TCP communication in Rust. As you continue your journey in networking with Rust, you'll explore more advanced concepts such as handling multiple connections, working with asynchronous tasks, and building robust applications that leverage the power and safety of Rust.

# Exploring Rust's Standard Library for Networking

In this chapter, we will explore Rust's standard library for networking, covering its key components, how to create networked applications, and best practices in the context of network programming.

## Understanding Rust's Standard Library for Networking

Rust provides a module for networking under `std::net`, which includes essential types and functions for creating TCP and UDP sockets, managing IP addresses, and handling network streams. The primary types in this module are:
```

`TcpStream` and `TcpListener`: For establishing TCP connections.

`UdpSocket`: For working with UDP connections.

`SocketAddr`: For representing an IP address and port combination. ### TCP Sockets

TcpStream

The `TcpStream` type represents a connection to a remote socket over TCP. It allows you to read and write data, ensuring reliable transmission of bytes between the client and server.

Here's an example of creating a TCP client that connects to a server:

```rust
use std::net::TcpStream; use std::io::{self, Write};

fn main() -> io::Result<()> {

// Attempt to connect to the server

let mut stream = TcpStream::connect("127.0.0.1:8080")?;


// Send data to the server stream.write_all(b"Hello, server!")?;


Ok(())

}
```

In this example, we connect to a server running on `localhost` at port `8080` and send a simple message.

TcpListener

The `TcpListener` type is used on the server side to listen for incoming TCP connections. It binds to a local socket address and waits for clients to connect.

Here's how to set up a simple TCP server:

```rust
use std::net::{TcpListener, TcpStream}; use std::io::{self, Read};

fn handle_client(mut stream: TcpStream) { let mut buffer = [0; 512];

let bytes_read = stream.read(&mut buffer).unwrap();

println!("Received:                    {}",
String::from_utf8_lossy(&buffer[0..bytes_read]));

}

fn main() -> io::Result<()> {

let listener = TcpListener::bind("127.0.0.1:8080")?;

for stream in listener.incoming() { match stream {

Ok(stream) => {

// Handle the client connection in a separate thread
handle_client(stream);

}

Err(e) => {

eprintln!("Failed to accept a connection: {}", e);

}
```

```
    }
  }
  Ok(())
}
```

This server listens for incoming connections, reads data sent by clients, and prints it to the console. ### UDP Sockets

The UDP protocol is connectionless and does not guarantee message delivery or order. Here, we introduce the `UdpSocket` type for sending and receiving messages over UDP.

Creating a UDP Client and Server

UDP sockets can be implemented similarly, but with a different approach. Here's a simple UDP client:

```rust
use std::net::UdpSocket;

fn main() {
    let socket = UdpSocket::bind("127.0.0.1:8080").expect("Couldn't bind to address");

    let msg = b"Hello, UDP!";
    socket.send_to(msg, "127.0.0.1:8081").expect("Failed to send data");
}
```

```
```

And the corresponding UDP server:

```rust
use std::net::UdpSocket;

fn main() {
    let socket = UdpSocket::bind("127.0.0.1:8081").expect("Couldn't bind to address");

    let mut buf = [0; 100];
    let (size, src) = socket.recv_from(&mut buf).expect("Failed to receive data");

    println!("Received from {}: {}", src, String::from_utf8_lossy(&buf[..size]));
}
```

In these examples, the server listens on one port (`8081`), while the client sends a message to it from another port (`8080`).

Asynchronous Networking with Tokio

While Rust's standard library provides sync network programming capabilities, for applications requiring high concurrency, using an asynchronous approach is often preferable. The Rust ecosystem features various libraries for asynchronous programming, with `Tokio` being one of the most popular.

Tokio provides asynchronous I/O, timers, and networking capabilities that integrate seamlessly with Rust's existing ecosystem. Here's a brief example of a simple TCP server using Tokio:

```rust
use tokio::net::{TcpListener, TcpStream}; use tokio::prelude::*;

async fn handle_client(stream: TcpStream) { let mut buffer = [0; 1024];

let n = stream.read(&mut buffer).await.unwrap(); println!("Received: {}", String::from_utf8_lossy(&buffer[..n]));

}

#[tokio::main] async fn main() {

let listener = TcpListener::bind("127.0.0.1:8080").await.unwrap();

loop {

let (stream, _) = listener.accept().await.unwrap(); tokio::spawn(handle_client(stream));

}

}
```

With asynchronous code, you can handle many connections simultaneously without blocking the main thread, making it suitable for applications that need to handle a high volume of network interactions.

Best Practices for Networking in Rust

Error Handling: Always handle potential errors gracefully. Rust's `Result` type provides a powerful way to handle errors effectively.

Keep Connections Alive: Implementing timeouts and connection management is essential in a network application, preventing stale connections and resource leaks.

Use Asynchronous Libraries for Concurrency: When building scalable applications, prefer asynchronous libraries and patterns, which allow handling numerous connections efficiently.

Security Considerations: Always consider security aspects such as input validation, encryption (e.g., using TLS), and safeguarding against common vulnerabilities like injection attacks.

Testing: Test your networking code rigorously. Network errors can be unpredictable, so unit tests and integration tests help ensure your code handles various scenarios.

By understanding and leveraging `std::net`, you can create robust applications efficiently. Moreover, for applications requiring high performance and concurrency, combining Rust's networking capabilities with asynchronous libraries like Tokio can significantly enhance your application's responsiveness and scalability.

Chapter 4: Building TCP Servers and Clients

TCP is one of the core protocols in the Internet Protocol Suite, and it provides a reliable, ordered, and error-checked delivery of a stream of data between applications. Understanding how to implement TCP servers and clients is essential for networking in languages such as Python, Java, or C++.

4.1 Understanding TCP

Before diving into the coding aspects, let's first understand some key attributes of TCP:

Connection-oriented: TCP establishes a connection before sending data, ensuring both parties are ready and agree on parameters.

Reliability: It guarantees the delivery of packets in the correct order. If packets are lost or received out of order, TCP is responsible for retransmitting them.

Flow Control: TCP uses flow control mechanisms to ensure that a sender does not overwhelm a receiver with too much data at once.

Congestion Control: TCP monitors network conditions and adjusts the rate of data transmission as necessary to prevent congestion.

These features make TCP suitable for applications like web browsing, file transfers, and other scenarios where reliability and order are critical.

4.2 Setting Up the Development Environment

To begin building our TCP servers and clients, you need to

have a suitable programming environment set up. For this chapter, we'll use Python due to its simplicity and readability. However, similar concepts translate well across languages.

Required Packages You will need:

Python 3.x installed on your machine.

Basic knowledge of Python syntax.

Once you have Python set up, you can create your Python files for the server and client implementations. ## 4.3 Building a TCP Server

Let's start by building a basic TCP server. The server will listen for incoming connections from clients, accept them, and then interact by sending and receiving messages.

Sample TCP Server Code

```python
import socket

def start_server(host='127.0.0.1', port=65432):
    # Create a socket object
    server_socket = socket.socket(socket.AF_INET, socket.SOCK_STREAM)


    # Bind the socket to the address and port
    server_socket.bind((host, port))
    # Enable the server to accept connections (set the max backlog of 5)
    server_socket.listen(5)
    print(f"Server started at {host}:{port}")
    while True:
```

```
# Wait for a client connection  client_socket, addr =
server_socket.accept() print(f"Connection from {addr}")

# Communicate with the client try:

message              =              "Hello,              Client!"
client_socket.sendall(message.encode())          data          =
client_socket.recv(1024)

print(f"Received from client: {data.decode()}") except
Exception as e:

print(f"Error: {e}") finally:

# Close the client socket client_socket.close()

if __name__ == "__main__":

start_server()
```
` ` `

Key Components of the Server Code

Socket Creation: `socket.socket()` creates a new socket using the Internet address family (AF_INET) and TCP (SOCK_STREAM).

Binding: The server binds to an IP address and port using `bind()`.

Listening: The server listens for incoming connections with `listen()`.

Accepting Connections: The server accepts client connections and creates a new socket for the connection via the `accept()` method.

Sending and Receiving Data: The server sends and receives messages using `sendall()` and `recv()`.

Closing Connections: Finally, it's essential to clean up by closing client sockets after finishing the communication.

4.4 Building a TCP Client

Now that we have a server, let's create a client that will connect to the server, send a message, and print the response.

Sample TCP Client Code

```python
import socket

def start_client(host='127.0.0.1', port=65432):
    # Create a socket object
    client_socket = socket.socket(socket.AF_INET, socket.SOCK_STREAM)

    # Connect to the server
    client_socket.connect((host, port))
    print(f"Connected to server at {host}:{port}")

    # Receive data from the server
    data = client_socket.recv(1024)
    print(f"Received from server: {data.decode()}")

    # Send data to the server
    message = "Hello, Server!"
    client_socket.sendall(message.encode())


    # Close the socket
    client_socket.close()

if __name__ == "__main__":
    start_client()
```

Key Components of the Client Code

Socket Creation: Similar to the server, a socket object is created with `socket.socket()`.

Connecting: The client connects to the server using `connect()`.

Data Communication: The client receives data from the server and sends a message back.

Closing the Connection: The client socket is closed after communication is completed. ## 4.5 Testing the TCP Server and Client

To test the implementation, you can run the server script first. Open a terminal window and execute the server code. Then, open another terminal window to run the client code. Once you run the client script, you should see messages being exchanged between the server and the client.

4.6 Enhancing the TCP Application

The current implementation of the server and client is quite basic. To enhance the application, consider the following:

Threading or Asynchronous I/O: Use threading or async methods to handle multiple client connections simultaneously.

Error Handling: Implement more robust error handling to manage scenarios like failed connections.

Data Serialization: Use serialization methods (like JSON) for complex data exchanges.

Security: Implement encryption (e.g., SSL/TLS) for

data privacy, especially when dealing with sensitive information.

We explored the fundamental concepts of TCP and how to manage connections and data communication. Understanding TCP is crucial for developing networked applications, and this knowledge can easily be applied across various programming languages.

Creating a Simple TCP Client in Rust

TCP (Transmission Control Protocol) is a fundamental protocol that forms the backbone of most internet communications. A client connects to a server, sends a request (often over a TCP socket), and waits for a response. Rust, with its focus on safety and performance, provides excellent capabilities for networking tasks.

Setting Up Your Rust Environment

Before we dive into coding, ensure you have Rust installed on your machine. If you haven't already installed Rust, you can do so by following these steps:

Open your command-line interface (CLI).

Run the following command to download and install Rust:

```bash
curl --proto '=https' --tlsv1.2 -sSf https://sh.rustup.rs | sh
```

Once the installation is complete, ensure that your Rust installation works by checking the version:

```bash
```

```
rustc --version
```

Creating a New Project

To create a new Rust project, we will use Cargo, Rust's package manager and build system. Open your CLI and run the following command:

```bash
cargo new tcp_client cd tcp_client
```

This command creates a new directory named `tcp_client` containing a basic Rust project structure. ## Adding Dependencies

For basic TCP client functionality, we will use the `std::net` module, which is part of Rust's standard library. Thus, we don't need to add external dependencies to our `Cargo.toml` file.

Writing the TCP Client

Open the `src/main.rs` file in your favorite text editor. We will build a simple TCP client that connects to a server and sends a message. For illustration, we will connect to `example.com` on port `80` (HTTP).

Here's a simple example of what your `main.rs` should look like:

```rust
use std::io::{self, Write, Read};

use std::net::{TcpStream, ToSocketAddrs};
```

```
fn main() -> io::Result<()> {

// Define the address of the server to connect to let
server_address = "example.com:80";

// Attempt to connect to the specified address

let mut stream = TcpStream::connect(server_address)?;

// The message we want to send to the server

let request = "GET / HTTP/1.0\r\nHost:
example.com\r\n\r\n";

// Send the request to the server
stream.write_all(request.as_bytes())?;

// Prepare a buffer to hold the server's response let mut
response = Vec::new();

// Read the response from the server
stream.read_to_end(&mut response)?;

// Print the server's response

println!("Response from server:\n{}",
String::from_utf8_lossy(&response));

Ok(())

}
```
```

### Code Breakdown

**Imports**: We import necessary types from the
standard library. `TcpStream` is used for TCP
communication, while `Write` and `Read` traits allow us
to send and receive data over the TCP stream.

**Main Function**: The main entry point of our
```

application returns a standard `Result` type to handle potential errors that might occur during TCP operations.

Connecting to the Server: We define the server address we want to connect to (`example.com` on port `80`). We use `TcpStream::connect` to establish a connection.

Sending Data: We prepare an HTTP GET request as a string and send it using `write_all`. This method sends all bytes of the request until the operation is complete.

Receiving Data: We read the server's response into a buffer using `read_to_end`, which reads all the bytes until the stream is closed.

Printing the Response: Finally, we convert the received bytes to a string and print them to the console.

Running the TCP Client

To run your TCP client, ensure you are in the `tcp_client` directory and execute:

```bash
bash cargo run
```

You should see the raw HTTP response returned by the server printed to your console.

Error Handling

In production code, robust error handling is vital. The example provided is basic and doesn't anticipate all possible errors. To enhance this, you might want to use the `Result` returned by methods to provide user-friendly error messages. Here's a revised version of the `main` function that includes simple error handling:

```rust
fn main() { match run() {

Ok(()) => println!("Successfully communicated with the server."), Err(e) => eprintln!("An error occurred: {}", e),

}

}

fn run() -> io::Result<()> {

// The same contents as our first main function...

}
```

Using `match` allows the program to handle success and failure gracefully.

We covered the basics of making a connection, sending requests, and handling responses. The Rust programming language provides robust tools for building efficient and secure networking applications, and mastering these tools empowers you to develop reliable software.

Implementing a Robust TCP Server

One of the areas where Rust shines is in network programming, particularly with its strong emphasis on safety and concurrency. In this chapter, we will explore how to implement a robust TCP server using Rust. We will cover setting up the basic TCP server structure, handling multiple connections concurrently, ensuring error handling, and emphasizing performance considerations.

Setting Up the Environment

Before delving into the implementation, ensure you have Rust installed on your system. You can install Rust using the official installer, `rustup`, which sets up the compiler and required tools. Load the Rust compiler and package manager by running the following command in your terminal:

```bash
curl --proto '=https' --tlsv1.2 -sSf https://sh.rustup.rs | sh
```

After installation, create a new Rust project:

```bash
cargo new tcp_server cd tcp_server
```

The Basic TCP Server Structure

With our Rust project ready, let's build a simple TCP server. We'll use the `std::net` module in Rust for networking functionality. Here's a minimal implementation:

```rust
use std::net::{TcpListener, TcpStream}; use std::io::{Read, Write};

use std::thread;

fn handle_client(mut stream: TcpStream) { let mut buffer = [0; 1024];

match stream.read(&mut buffer) { Ok(bytes_read) => {

println!("Received          message:          {:?}",
```

70

```
    String::from_utf8_lossy(&buffer[..bytes_read]));
    write_response(&mut stream).expect("Failed to send
    response");
}
Err(e) => eprintln!("Failed to read from client: {}", e),
    }
}

fn write_response(stream: &mut TcpStream) ->
std::io::Result<()> { const RESPONSE: &str = "Hello
from        Rust        TCP        server!";
stream.write(RESPONSE.as_bytes())?;

stream.flush()?;

Ok(())
}

fn main() {

let              listener              =
TcpListener::bind("127.0.0.1:7878").expect("Could    not
bind to address"); println!("Server listening on port
7878");

for stream in listener.incoming() { match stream {

Ok(stream) => {

thread::spawn(|| handle_client(stream));

}
Err(e) => eprintln!("Failed to accept connection: {}", e),

}
}
```

```
}
```
```
### Breakdown of the Code

**Imports**: We import necessary modules for networking and I/O operations.

**`handle_client` Function**: This function reads data from a connected client and responds with a welcome message.

**`write_response` Function**: Sends a predefined response back to the client.

**`main` Function**: Binds the server to a given IP and port, listens for incoming connections, and spawns a new thread to handle each client.

## Concurrent Connection Handling

Concurrency is crucial for a TCP server, allowing it to handle multiple connections simultaneously without blocking. In our example, we utilize Rust's threads for this purpose. Each incoming connection spawns a new thread that handles the communication with the client. This prevents any single client interaction from blocking others, hence making the server robust.

### Advanced Concurrency with Async

As an alternative to using threads, Rust also provides asynchronous programming capabilities. By utilizing the `tokio` runtime, we can handle connections in a non-blocking manner. Here's an example using async/await syntax:

```rust

```rust
use tokio::net::{TcpListener, TcpStream};
use tokio::io::{AsyncReadExt, AsyncWriteExt};
#[tokio::main] async fn main() {
let listener = TcpListener::bind("127.0.0.1:7878").await.expect("Could
not bind to address"); println!("Server listening on port
7878");
loop {
let (socket, _) = listener.accept().await.expect("Failed to
accept connection"); tokio::spawn(async move {
handle_client(socket).await;
});
}
}
async fn handle_client(mut socket: TcpStream) { let mut
buffer = [0; 1024];
match socket.read(&mut buffer).await { Ok(bytes_read)
=> {
println!("Received message: {:?}",
String::from_utf8_lossy(&buffer[..bytes_read]));
write_response(&mut socket).await.expect("Failed to
send response");
}
Err(e) => eprintln!("Failed to read from client: {}", e),
}
}
```

```rust
async fn write_response(socket: &mut TcpStream) ->
std::io::Result<()> { const RESPONSE: &str = "Hello from
Rust asynchronous TCP server!";
socket.write_all(RESPONSE.as_bytes()).await?;

Ok(())

}
```
```

This implementation uses asynchronous handling and is more scalable for high traffic scenarios. With

`tokio`, we minimize thread spawning and keep our resource consumption lower. ## Error Handling and Robustness

Robustness in a TCP server hinges on effective error handling. All network communication can fail, and proper handling ensures that the server remains operational even when faced with issues. In our implementations, we've included `match` statements to gracefully handle errors during reading and writing.

For a production-grade server, extending on this idea could include logging errors, retrying connections, or implementing a circuit breaker pattern to temporarily halt requests if issues persist.

## Performance Considerations

When designing a TCP server, performance is a critical aspect. Here are some tips for ensuring high performance:

**Connection Pooling**: For certain applications, maintaining persistent connections can reduce connection overhead.
```

Load Balancing: For high traffic scenarios, distribute requests across multiple server instances.

Backpressure Mechanism: If the server is overwhelmed, implement backpressure strategies to slow down incoming connections rather than rejecting them outright.

Benchmarking: Utilize Rust's built-in profiling tools to measure performance and identify bottlenecks.

By leveraging Rust's safety and concurrency features, along with a strong focus on error handling and performance considerations, we can build servers that are both efficient and reliable.

Chapter 5: Working with UDP Protocols

User Datagram Protocol (UDP) is one of the core protocols of the Internet Protocol (IP) suite. Its importance in various applications such as streaming media, online gaming, and real-time communications is undeniable due to its low-latency characteristics. While TCP (Transmission Control Protocol) offers reliable communication, UDP sacrifices reliability for speed, making it ideal for applications where timely delivery is more critical than absolute arrival accuracy. This chapter delves into the workings of the UDP protocol, its features, advantages, and various applications, along with practical examples of its implementation.

5.1 Understanding UDP

UDP operates at the transport layer of the Internet Protocol Suite, just like TCP, but it does so without establishing a connection and without guaranteeing delivery. This combination results in a lightweight protocol that allows applications to send messages, or "datagrams," with minimal overhead. UDP includes features that allow it to transmit data efficiently, such as:

No connection establishment: UDP is a connectionless protocol. There is no need for a handshake before sending data, allowing for faster message transmission.

Less overhead: The lack of connection control means UDP has lower overhead compared to TCP. The header is minimal, usually consisting of just eight bytes, thus maximizing the amount of payload data that can be sent.

Best-effort delivery: UDP does not guarantee the delivery of packets. Lost packets are not retransmitted automatically, and there's no built-in mechanism for error correction or ordering. It's up to the application to handle these potential issues if they matter for the context.

5.2 UDP Packet Structure

A UDP packet consists of four key fields in its header:

Source Port (16 bits): This is the port number used by the source application to send the data.

Destination Port (16 bits): This is the port number on the destination device where the data is to be sent, allowing multiple applications to communicate over the same IP address.

Length (16 bits): The total length of the UDP packet, including the header and the data payload.

Checksum (16 bits): This optional field is used for error-checking the header and data. It can help identify corrupted packets.

The simplicity of the UDP header facilitates quick processing by routers and devices across a network. ## 5.3 Advantages of Using UDP

5.3.1 Speed

The most significant advantage of UDP is its speed. Applications that rely on real-time data transmission benefit from the reduced latency since UDP skips the connection establishment and teardown phases inherent in TCP.

5.3.2 Reduced Overhead

Due to its lightweight header and lack of connection management, UDP offers reduced overhead, allowing for efficient use of bandwidth and quick packet dispatch.

5.3.3 Suitable for Real-Time Applications

UDP is preferred for protocols that require fast transmission rates over perfect delivery. Applications such as Voice over IP (VoIP), video streaming, and online gaming often prioritize speed and can tolerate some data loss.

5.4 Disadvantages of Using UDP

Despite its advantages, UDP comes with certain challenges:

5.4.1 No Reliability

Unlike TCP, UDP does not guarantee that packets will arrive at their destination. If packet loss occurs during transmission, there is no mechanism for retransmission or error correction.

5.4.2 No Order Guarantee

Packets sent via UDP can arrive out of order. It is the application's responsibility to handle proper sequencing if the order of message delivery is crucial.

5.4.3 Congestion Control

UDP does not provide any built-in congestion control mechanisms. Therefore, it may exacerbate congestion in network traffic, especially during peak usage.

5.5 Use Cases of UDP

Several applications utilize UDP due to its characteristics, including:

5.5.1 Streaming Media

Protocols like Real-Time Streaming Protocol (RTSP) harness the capabilities of UDP, enabling rapid transmission of audio and video data streams without delays.

5.5.2 Online Gaming

In fast-paced online games, even minor delays can ruin player experience. UDP ensures timely delivery of game state updates, which is crucial for real-time interaction.

5.5.3 Voice and Video Calls

VoIP applications like Skype and video conferencing platforms employ UDP to maintain the conversational flow, where latency is more critical than reliability.

5.5.4 Domain Name System (DNS)

DNS queries utilize UDP for quicker responses, as the protocol's speed is usually more critical than the reliability of these requests.

5.6 Implementing UDP in Network Programming ### 5.6.1 Basic UDP Socket Programming

To illustrate how to work with UDP, let's consider a brief example using Python's socket library. Below is a simple client-server implementation using UDP.

UDP Server Example

```python
import socket

def udp_server():

    server_socket = socket.socket(socket.AF_INET, socket.SOCK_DGRAM)
    server_socket.bind(('localhost',
```

5000)) # Bind to localhost and port 5000

print("UDP server is up and listening...") while True:

message, client_address = server_socket.recvfrom(1024) # Receive up to 1024 bytes

print(f"Received message: {message.decode()} from {client_address}")
server_socket.sendto(b'Acknowledged', client_address) # Send acknowledgment

udp_server()
```

#### UDP Client Example

```python import socket

def udp_client(message):

client_socket = socket.socket(socket.AF_INET, socket.SOCK_DGRAM)
client_socket.sendto(message.encode(), ('localhost', 5000)) # Send message to server acknowledgment, _ = client_socket.recvfrom(1024)

print(f"Server response: {acknowledgment.decode()}")


udp_client("Hello, UDP server!")
```

5.6.2 Considerations for Application Design

When designing applications to use UDP, developers should consider:

Data Integrity: Implement custom checks or
```

sequences if ensuring data integrity is necessary for your use case.

Packet Loss Handling: Develop strategies for handling cases of packet loss and possible recovery mechanism if critical data does not arrive.

Latency Sensitivity: Determine the acceptable trade-off between speed and reliability based on application requirements.

While it lacks the reliability features of TCP, its lightweight nature and flexibility make it ideal for real-time services. Understanding when and how to utilize UDP can enable developers to build high-performance applications tailored to user expectations and real-time data demands.

Developing Lightweight UDP Clients

In this chapter, we focus on developing lightweight UDP clients using Rust, a systems programming language renowned for its emphasis on safety and performance. This exploration will cover understanding the UDP model, utilizing Rust's standard library for network programming, and implementing a simple UDP client while highlighting best practices and optimization techniques.

Understanding UDP

UDP is a connectionless protocol that allows for sending messages, called datagrams, between host devices on an IP network. Unlike TCP, UDP does not guarantee message delivery, order of messages, or error checking, making it an excellent choice for applications where speed is crucial, such as gaming, VoIP, and real-time streaming.

Key Characteristics of UDP

Connectionless: There's no need to establish a connection before sending data.

Lightweight: UDP headers are smaller, resulting in less overhead than TCP.

No reliability guarantees: There's no automatic retransmission of lost packets, making UDP unsuitable for applications that require reliable transmission.

Why Rust for UDP Clients?

Rust has gained popularity among developers for its memory safety features and zero-cost abstractions, making it an excellent choice for system programming and network applications. Its strong type system, along with the built-in concurrency features, allows for safe, efficient, and performant code that can directly manage system resources.

Advantages of Rust

Memory Safety: Rust's borrowing and ownership rules prevent data races and other common bugs.

Concurrency: Rust makes it easier to write concurrent programs with safe access to shared resources.

Performance: Rust's performance is comparable to C and C++, making it suitable for high- performance networking tasks.

Setting Up the Development Environment

Before diving into the code, you need to set up your

development environment. Ensure you have the latest version of Rust installed. You can get it through `rustup`, Rust's official installer:

```bash
curl --proto '=https' --tlsv1.2 -sSf https://sh.rustup.rs | sh
```

After installation, verify it by running:

```bash
rustc --version
```

Creating a New Project

Use Cargo, Rust's package manager, to create a new project:

```bash
cargo new udp_client cd udp_client
```

This command generates a basic directory structure for a Rust project. ## Implementing a Lightweight UDP Client

Dependencies

For our lightweight UDP client, we will utilize Rust's standard library `std::net`, which provides straightforward abstractions for TCP and UDP networking.

Basic UDP Client Code

Here's a simple implementation of a UDP client that sends a message to a server and waits for a response:

```rust
use std::net::{UdpSocket, SocketAddr}; use std::str;

fn main() -> std::io::Result<()> {

// Binding the UDP socket to a specific address and port
let socket = UdpSocket::bind("127.0.0.1:0")?;
println!("Using local address: {}", socket.local_addr()?);

// The address of the server we will send a message to

let server_address: SocketAddr = "127.0.0.1:12345".parse().unwrap();

// Message to be sent to the server

let message = b"Hello, UDP Server!";
socket.send_to(message, &server_address)?;

// Buffer to hold the response from the server let mut buf = [0; 1024];


// Receiving the response

let (number_of_bytes, src_addr) = socket.recv_from(&mut buf)?; println!("Received {} bytes from {:?}: {}", number_of_bytes, src_addr,

str::from_utf8(&buf[..number_of_bytes]).unwrap());
Ok(())
}
```

Code Explanation

Binding the Socket: We bind the UDP socket using `UdpSocket::bind` to a local address. By specifying `0`

84

for the port, the system will assign an available port dynamically.

Sending Data: The message is sent using `send_to`, which takes the message bytes and the server address as arguments.

Receiving Data: The client uses `recv_from` to receive messages from the server. It fills the buffer and returns the number of bytes received and the source address of the sender.

Error Handling: Rust's powerful error handling is evident here with `Result` types, ensuring that potential errors in binding, sending, and receiving are handled safely.

Best Practices and Optimization

When developing UDP applications, particularly with Rust, consider the following best practices:

Avoiding Large Buffers: Allocate buffers based on expected maximum sizes to reduce memory usage.

Timeouts: Since UDP does not guarantee delivery, consider implementing timeouts for receiving messages.

Connection Management: Properly manage the socket's lifecycle, ensuring it closes when no longer needed.

Concurrency: Use Rust's concurrency features to handle multiple clients and processes simultaneously without data races, such as using threads or the async/await paradigm.

In a world driven by performance, mastering UDP client development in Rust opens many opportunities for building high-speed, responsive applications. In the upcoming chapters, we will delve into more advanced UDP constructs, including multicast, error handling, and using asynchronous patterns for more complex concurrency scenarios.

Handling Packet Loss and Reliability

Regardless of the cause, the need for reliable communication between systems remains paramount. Rust, with its emphasis on safety and concurrency, provides developers with robust tools to build reliable networking applications.

In this chapter, we will explore the principles of handling packet loss, strategies for ensuring reliability, and how to implement these concepts effectively in Rust. We will examine error handling, retries, and acknowledgments, and we will conclude with practical code examples.

2. Understanding Packet Loss ### 2.1 What is Packet Loss?

Packet loss refers to the failure of one or more packets to reach their intended destination. This can result in degraded performance, increased latency, or even the inability to establish a connection. In real-time applications, such as video conferencing and online gaming, packet loss can severely impact user experience.

2.2 Causes of Packet Loss

The causes of packet loss can be broadly categorized into:

Network Congestion: An overloaded network might drop packets to cope with high traffic.

Hardware Failures: Failing routers and switches can lead to data loss.

Software Issues: Bugs in network drivers or applications can result in lost packets.

Environmental Factors: Wireless networks can be impacted by physical obstacles and interference. ### 2.3 Consequences of Packet Loss

The consequences of packet loss vary depending on the application. For example:

In TCP: The protocol employs retransmission strategies, ensuring that lost packets are resent, which can lead to reduced throughput.

In UDP: Packet loss can be more pronounced, as the protocol does not guarantee delivery, possibly leading to incomplete media streams or lost data.

3. Strategies for Ensuring Reliability ### 3.1 Error Handling

Effective error handling is the foundation of creating reliable network applications. In Rust, the `Result` and `Option` types are used extensively to convey the success or failure of operations. This allows developers to handle potential errors gracefully and write more robust code.

3.2 Retries and Exponential Backoff

When a packet is lost, one common strategy is to implement a retry mechanism. The idea is to resend the lost packet after a certain timeout. To avoid congesting the network further, implementing an exponential backoff strategy is recommended. This means that the wait time between retries increases exponentially, giving the network time to recover.

3.3 Acknowledgments

Acknowledgments (ACKs) are essential for reliable communication. The sender can track which packets have been received successfully and retransmit any that have not been acknowledged. In UDP-based applications, implementing a lightweight acknowledgment mechanism provides a balance between reliability and performance.

4. Implementing Reliability in Rust

Let's look at how we can implement these principles in Rust. We will create a simple TCP-like client and server model that demonstrates the handling of packet loss and reliability.

4.1 TCP Client Example

Here's a basic conceptual implementation of a TCP-like client that includes retries and acknowledgments:

```rust
use std::io::{self, Write, Read};

use std::net::{TcpStream, SocketAddr}; use std::time::{Duration, Instant};

use std::thread;

const MAX_RETRIES: usize = 5;

fn send_packet(stream: &mut TcpStream, packet: &[u8]) -> io::Result<()> { stream.write_all(packet)?;
```

```rust
let mut ack = [0; 2];

let start = Instant::now();

// Retry logic with exponential backoff for attempt in
1..=MAX_RETRIES {

stream.set_read_timeout(Some(Duration::from_secs(2)))
?; match stream.read(&mut ack) {

Ok(n)  if  n  >  0  &&  ack  ==  b"OK"  =>  {
println!("Acknowledgment  received  for  packet:  {:?}",
packet); return Ok(());
}

_ => {

println!("No acknowledgment, retrying... Attempt {}/{}",
attempt,     MAX_RETRIES);     let     wait_time     =
Duration::from_secs(2_u64.pow(attempt     as     u32));
thread::sleep(wait_time);
}
}
}

Err(io::Error::new(io::ErrorKind::TimedOut, "Failed to
receive acknowledgment"))
}

fn main() -> io::Result<()> { let addr = "127.0.0.1:7878";

let mut stream = TcpStream::connect(addr)?; let packet =
b"Hello, World!";
```

```rust
match send_packet(&mut stream, packet) { Ok(()) =>
println!("Packet sent successfully!"),

Err(e) => println!("Error sending packet: {:?}", e),

}


Ok(())

}
```

4.2 TCP Server Example

Now, let's create a simple server that listens for incoming packets and sends acknowledgments back.

```rust
use std::io::{self, Read, Write};

use std::net::{TcpListener, TcpStream};

fn handle_client(mut stream: TcpStream) ->
io::Result<()> { let mut buffer = [0; 1024];


loop {

let bytes_read = stream.read(&mut buffer)?; if bytes_read == 0 {

break; // Connection closed

}

println!("Received packet: {:?}", &buffer[..bytes_read]);
stream.write_all(b"OK")?; // Acknowledge receipt of packet
```

```
}
Ok(())
}
fn main() -> io::Result<()> {
let listener = TcpListener::bind("127.0.0.1:7878")?;

println!("Server listening on port 7878"); for stream in
listener.incoming() {
match stream { Ok(s) => {
handle_client(s)?;
}
Err(e) => {
println!("Connection failed: {:?}", e);
}
}
}
Ok(())
}
```
` ` `

Managing packet loss and ensuring reliability are crucial
components of network programming. In this chapter, we
discussed the nature of packet loss, its consequences, and
strategies for ensuring reliable communication using Rust.
With Rust's powerful type system and concurrency
features, developers can build robust networking

applications that handle packet loss gracefully.

Chapter 6: Leveraging Asynchronous Programming

In this chapter, we will explore the core concepts of asynchronous programming in Rust, the tools and libraries available, and practical examples to help you leverage this powerful feature effectively.

6.1 Understanding Asynchronous Programming in Rust

At its core, asynchronous programming allows you to write code that can initiate tasks that will complete in the future while continuing to operate without waiting for them to finish. In contrast to synchronous code, where operations occur one after the other, asynchronous code can handle multiple tasks at the same time, making it more efficient.

Rust's approach to asynchronous programming is centered around the concepts of **`async`** functions,

`await` expressions, and the concept of futures. The `async` keyword enables you to define a function that returns a **Future**, which represents a value that will be available at some point.

Here's a simple example of an asynchronous function:

```rust
async fn fetch_data() -> String {
//        Simulate      a       web       request
delay_for(Duration::from_secs(2)).await; "Data from the server".to_string()
}
```

```
` ` `
```

In this example, `fetch_data` is an asynchronous function that simulates fetching data by delaying for two seconds.

6.2 The `Future` Trait

In Rust, the `Future` trait is a fundamental building block for asynchronous programming. Any value that implements this trait represents a computation that may not have completed yet. To create a future, you can use the `async` keyword on a function.

Here's how we can define and use a future:

```rust
use std::future::Future;

fn perform_async_task() -> impl Future<Output = i32> {
async {
// Simulate some computation 42
}
}
```

In this snippet, `perform_async_task` returns a value that implements `Future`, which will eventually hold an `i32`.

6.3 Using `async` and `await`

The `await` keyword is used to yield control back to the executor until the `Future` is ready. It allows you to work with asynchronous code in a way that feels synchronous. This method is crucial because it helps maintain readable code structure.

Here's an example demonstrating the use of `async` and `await`:

```rust
use tokio;

#[tokio::main] async fn main() {

let data = fetch_data().await; println!("Received: {}", data);

}
```

In this code, we use the Tokio runtime to drive our asynchronous functions. The `#[tokio::main]` macro sets up the async runtime, allowing us to call `await` within the `main` function.

6.4 The Tokio Runtime

One of the most popular libraries for asynchronous programming in Rust is **Tokio**. It provides a runtime that executes asynchronous tasks and manages threads and I/O operations efficiently. Tokio enables developers to build systems capable of handling many simultaneous connections with minimal overhead.

To use Tokio, you will need to add it to your `Cargo.toml`:

```toml
[dependencies]

tokio = { version = "1", features = ["full"] }
```

A basic example using Tokio could look like the following:

```rust
```

```rust
use tokio::time::{sleep, Duration};

async fn async_task(name: &str) { println!("Task {}
started.", name); sleep(Duration::from_secs(2)).await;
println!("Task {} completed.", name);
}

#[tokio::main] async fn main() {

let task1 = async_task("A"); let task2 = async_task("B");


// Run both tasks concurrently tokio::join!(task1, task2);
}
```

In this example, both tasks are started concurrently, and
the program will wait for both to complete before it exits.

6.5 Handling Errors in Asynchronous Code

Error handling in asynchronous programming requires
attention to detail, especially because futures can fail.
Rust's `Result` type continues to serve its purpose in
async functions. It's important to propagate errors
correctly using the `?` operator.

Here's an example demonstrating how to handle errors in
an async function:

```rust
async fn fetch_data_with_error() -> Result<String,
&'static str> {

// Simulate an error during fetching Err("Network error")
}
```

```
#[tokio::main] async fn main() {

match fetch_data_with_error().await { Ok(data) =>
println!("Received: {}", data),

Err(e) => eprintln!("Error fetching data: {}", e),

}

}
```
` ` `

In this function, if an error occurs, it is propagated up to the caller, allowing for appropriate error handling. ## 6.6 Best Practices in Asynchronous Rust

Use the Right Runtime: Choose a runtime that suits your application needs. While Tokio is powerful and full-featured, alternatives like async-std or smol may fit simpler use cases.

Minimize Blocking Calls: Avoid calls that block the async runtime. If you need to perform CPU- bound computations, consider offloading those tasks to a separate thread using a thread pool.

Error Handling: Use the standard error propagation techniques available in Rust to handle errors gracefully.

Testing Asynchronous Code: Keep in mind that testing async functions requires some additional setup. Use frameworks like `tokio::test` for unit testing async code.

Be Mindful of Memory: Understand how futures retain memory and ensure that you manage lifetimes prudently to avoid leaks or dangling references.

By leveraging the `async` and `await` syntax, the

`Future` trait, and robust libraries like Tokio, developers can create systems that handle concurrency seamlessly. As you continue your journey in Rust programming, mastering asynchronous techniques will be essential for building scalable and responsive applications.

Async/Await in Rust: Basics and Benefits

Rust, a systems programming language known for its memory safety guarantees and zero-cost abstractions, has embraced asynchronous programming with the async/await syntax. This chapter explores the basics of async/await in Rust and highlights its benefits for network programming.

Understanding Asynchronous Programming

Asynchronous programming allows applications to perform tasks without blocking the main execution thread. This is particularly useful in I/O-bound operations, like network requests, where waiting for responses can waste valuable processing time. Traditional threading models can often be resource-intensive, resulting in performance bottlenecks.

Rust's async/await model introduces a more efficient approach by enabling developers to write non-blocking code that reads like synchronous code. This drastically simplifies the process of managing concurrency while maintaining the language's strong safety guarantees.

The Basics of Async/Await in Rust ### Setting Up an Async Environment

To utilize async/await in Rust, you will first need to set up an asynchronous runtime. The most commonly used runtimes include `tokio` and `async-std`. To get started with `tokio`, add the following dependency to your `Cargo.toml`:

```toml
[dependencies]
tokio = { version = "1", features = ["full"] }
```

Defining Asynchronous Functions

In Rust, you define an asynchronous function using the `async fn` syntax. This syntax indicates that the function will return a `Future`, which is a value that represents an asynchronous computation. For example:

```rust
use tokio::net::TcpStream;

async fn connect_to_server(address: &str) -> Result<TcpStream, std::io::Error> { let stream = TcpStream::connect(address).await?;

Ok(stream)

}
```

In this function, `connect_to_server` connects to a TCP server asynchronously. The `.await` keyword tells Rust that this function will pause until the `connect` call is complete without blocking the entire thread.

Executing Asynchronous Code

To execute asynchronous code, you need to run it within an async runtime. Here's a simple example:

99

```rust
#[tokio::main] async fn main() {
    match connect_to_server("127.0.0.1:8080").await {
        Ok(stream) => println!("Connected to the server!"),
        Err(e) => eprintln!("Failed to connect: {}", e),
    }
}
```

The `#[tokio::main]` macro sets up a Tokio runtime and allows `main` to be asynchronous. When `main` is called, it can await other asynchronous functions.

Benefits of Async/Await for Network Programming
Improved Performance and Scalability

One of the primary benefits of using async/await is the ability to perform non-blocking operations without the overhead of managing threads. This is particularly useful in network programming, where I/O operations may be latency-prone. An asynchronous system can handle multiple connections concurrently without requiring a separate thread for each one, thereby conserving system resources.

Simplified Code Structure

Async/await syntax makes the code easier to read and maintain compared to traditional callback-based or thread management models. This leads to more expressive and understandable code, allowing developers to focus on the logic of the application rather than the complexities of managing concurrency.

```rust
```

```rust
async fn fetch_data() -> Result<String, reqwest::Error> {
    let response = reqwest::get("https://api.example.com/data").await?; let data = response.text().await?;

    Ok(data)
}
```

In the example above, `fetch_data` demonstrates how asynchronous calls can be chained in a linear, intuitive manner, enhancing code clarity.

Error Handling

Rust's powerful error handling mechanisms, combined with async/await, facilitate effective management of errors that occur during asynchronous operations. Since the `Future` type implements the `Result` trait, it allows developers to handle errors cleanly within the async/await workflow.

Community and Ecosystem Support

The Rust community has embraced async programming, leading to robust libraries and frameworks that simplify the task of building asynchronous applications. Libraries like `tokio`, `async-std`, and `reqwest` have matured and are widely used in production environments for building scalable network applications.

With its numerous benefits—such as increased performance, clearer code structure, improved error handling, and extensive community support—adopting async/await can significantly enhance the robustness and efficiency of networked applications.

Using Tokio for High-Performance Networking

In the programming landscape, Rust has gained significant traction for its powerful performance and safety guarantees, making it a prime choice for building high-performance networking applications. Tokio, an asynchronous runtime for Rust, offers a robust framework for developing network services that take full advantage of Rust's capabilities. In this chapter, we will delve deep into how to utilize Tokio to create high- performance networking applications in Rust.

1. What is Tokio?

Tokio is an asynchronous runtime for the Rust programming language, designed for building fast and reliable network applications. Its key features include:

Non-blocking I/O: Tokio allows developers to handle multiple I/O operations concurrently without blocking the thread. This efficient approach maximizes resource utilization and enhances application performance.

Task scheduling: Tokio includes a lightweight task system that allows the execution of asynchronous tasks through a single-threaded or multi-threaded model, depending on the application's requirements.

Ecosystem of libraries: Tokio supports a range of libraries and utilities built around asynchronous programming, making it easier to interact with protocols, handle sockets, and manage streams.

2. Setting Up a Tokio Project

To start using Tokio in your Rust project, you first need to set up a new Rust project and include Tokio in your dependencies. Follow these steps:

Create a new Rust project:

```bash
cargo new tokio_networking cd tokio_networking
```

Add Tokio to your `Cargo.toml`:

Open `Cargo.toml` and add Tokio as a dependency. You may also want to include the `full` feature to access all components:

```toml [dependencies]
tokio = { version = "1", features = ["full"] }
```

Check your toolchain:

Ensure that you're using the stable version of Rust. Some Tokio features may require specific Rust versions.

3. Understanding Asynchronous Programming in Rust with Tokio

Asynchronous programming enables writing code that can perform multiple tasks at the same time without waiting for each task to complete. Tokio employs Rust's `async` and `await` syntax, making it more intuitive.

3.1. Async Functions

In Tokio, asynchronous functions are defined with the `async fn` syntax. Here's a simple example of an asynchronous function that simulates an I/O operation:

```rust
async fn perform_io_operation() {
// Simulate an I/O-bound operation println!("Performing I/O operation...");
}
```

3.2. Awaiting Futures

When calling an asynchronous function, it returns a `Future`. The actual operation won't occur until you `.await` it:

```rust #[tokio::main] async fn main() {
perform_io_operation().await;
}
```

The `#[tokio::main]` attribute transforms the main function to an asynchronous entry point for your application.

4. Building a Simple TCP Server

Let's create a simple TCP server using Tokio that listens for incoming connections and echoes received messages back to the client. This example highlights the non-blocking nature of Tokio's networking capabilities.

4.1. Creating the Server

Below is a basic implementation of an echo server:

```rust
```

```rust
use tokio::net::{TcpListener, TcpStream};

use tokio::io::{AsyncBufReadExt, AsyncWriteExt, BufReader};

async fn handle_client(stream: TcpStream) { let (reader, writer) = stream.into_split(); let mut reader = BufReader::new(reader); let mut buffer = String::new();

loop {

// Read a line from the client

match reader.read_line(&mut buffer).await { Ok(0) => break, // Connection closed Ok(_) => {

// Echo back the line

writer.write_all(buffer.as_bytes()).await.unwrap();
buffer.clear(); // Clear buffer for next use

}

Err(_) => {

eprintln!("Failed to read from client"); break;

}

}

}

}

#[tokio::main] async fn main() {

let listener = TcpListener::bind("127.0.0.1:8080").await.unwrap();
println!("Server is running on 127.0.0.1:8080");

loop {
```

```
let (stream, _) = listener.accept().await.unwrap();
tokio::spawn(handle_client(stream)); // Handle each
client in a new task
}
}
```
` ` `

4.2. Explanation of the Code

TcpListener: This listens for incoming TCP connections on the specified address.

Async I/O operations: The `read_line` and `write_all` methods provide non-blocking I/O.

Concurrency with tokio::spawn: Each client connection is handled in a separate task, allowing the server to maintain responsiveness.

5. High-Performance Considerations

When building high-performance networking applications, it's essential to consider several factors:

Efficient resource usage: Leverage Tokio's asynchronous capabilities to handle numerous connections without spawning a thread for each client.

Connection pooling: Reuse connections where applicable to reduce overhead.

Load balancing: Design your server architecture to balance the load among multiple instances efficiently.

Error handling: Implement comprehensive error handling to ensure reliability under varying network conditions.

We covered the essential concepts of asynchronous programming, set up a simple TCP echo server, and discussed performance considerations for real-world applications. Tokio's robust ecosystem and Rust's safety features make it an excellent choice for developers looking to create efficient, safe networking services.

Chapter 7: Securing Network Applications

This chapter delves into the vital aspects of securing network applications, exploring various threats, vulnerabilities, best practices, and the technologies that can help safeguard these critical systems.

Understanding the Threat Landscape

Before implementing any security measures, it is essential to understand the potential threats that network applications face. These threats can be categorized into several types:

1. **Malware Attacks**

Malware, including viruses, worms, and Trojans, can compromise an application's integrity by exploiting vulnerabilities. Once infiltrated, malware can steal sensitive information, disrupt operations, or even launch attacks on other systems.

2. **Denial of Service (DoS) Attacks**

DoS and Distributed Denial of Service (DDoS) attacks are designed to overwhelm an application with traffic, rendering it inoperable. These attacks can be devastating for businesses, leading to downtime and significant financial losses.

3. **Exploits and Vulnerabilities**

Software vulnerabilities can be exploited by attackers to gain unauthorized access or perform malicious actions. Common vulnerabilities include SQL injection, Cross-Site Scripting (XSS), and buffer overflows, which can compromise the security of network applications.

4. **Man-in-the-Middle (MitM) Attacks**

In MitM attacks, an attacker intercepts communication between two parties, allowing them to eavesdrop on or manipulate the data exchanged. This type of attack can severely compromise the confidentiality and integrity of the information transmitted.

5. **Insider Threats**

Not all security threats come from outside the organization. Insider threats, whether intentional or unintentional, can pose significant risks to network applications. Employees with access to sensitive data may mishandle it or fall victim to social engineering attacks.

Securing Network Applications: Best Practices

To mitigate the risks associated with these threats, organizations must adopt a comprehensive security strategy that encompasses various best practices:

1. **Secure Coding Practices**

Developers should adhere to secure coding guidelines to minimize vulnerabilities during the development phase. This includes input validation, proper error handling, and adhering to the principle of least privilege.

2. **Regular Security Audits and Testing**

Conducting regular security audits, vulnerability assessments, and penetration testing is crucial to identify and address weaknesses in network applications. These proactive measures can help organizations stay one step ahead of potential attackers.

3. **Implementing Authentication and Authorization Controls**

Strong authentication mechanisms, such as multi-factor authentication (MFA), and proper authorization protocols help ensure that only legitimate users gain access to network applications. Role-based access control (RBAC) can further limit user access according to their job responsibilities.

4. **Data Encryption**

Encrypting data both at rest and in transit protects sensitive information from unauthorized access. TLS (Transport Layer Security) should be employed to secure communications between clients and servers, while encryption standards such as AES can be utilized for stored data.

5. **Regular Updates and Patch Management**

Keeping software up-to-date and promptly applying security patches is essential for mitigating known vulnerabilities. Organizations should have a robust patch management process in place to ensure that all network applications are regularly updated.

6. **Incident Response Plan**

Having a well-defined incident response plan is critical for quickly addressing security breaches. This plan should outline the roles and responsibilities of team members, communication strategies, and steps to contain and remediate the attack.

Technologies for Securing Network Applications

Alongside best practices, several technologies can enhance

the security of network applications: ### 1. **Web Application Firewalls (WAFs)**

WAFs provide a barrier between web applications and potential threats, filtering and monitoring HTTP traffic to block malicious requests and prevent attacks such as SQL injection and XSS.

2. **Intrusion Detection and Prevention Systems (IDPS)**

These systems help monitor network traffic for suspicious activities, enabling organizations to detect and respond to potential threats in real-time.

3. **API Security Solutions**

As APIs become increasingly integral to network applications, securing them is essential. API security solutions can help protect against various threats, such as data breaches and improper access.

4. **Security Information and Event Management (SIEM)**

SIEM solutions aggregate and analyze security data from across the network, providing insights into potential threats and aiding in incident response.

The Road Ahead: Future Considerations

As technology evolves, so do the threats to network applications. Organizations must remain vigilant and adaptive in their security strategies. Emerging technologies like artificial intelligence (AI) and machine learning (ML) are beginning to play a significant role in detecting and combating cyber threats. However, the human element remains crucial—well-trained staff and a culture of security awareness within organizations can significantly enhance defenses against potential attacks.

By understanding the threat landscape, implementing best practices, leveraging technology, and fostering a security-conscious culture, organizations can better protect their network applications from an ever-evolving array of cyber threats. As we move forward in an increasingly interconnected world, prioritizing security in application development and management will be critical to sustaining trust and integrity in the digital realm.

Implementing TLS with Rustls

TLS achieves this through encryption, authentication, and integrity verification. As digital communication grows more complex and data breaches become more frequent, implementing TLS in your applications is crucial for safeguarding sensitive information.

In this chapter, we will dive into using Rustls, a modern TLS library in Rust, to secure your applications. Rustls is a Safe and Fast TLS 1.2 and 1.3 implementation written in Rust. It is designed to be simple and efficient, making it an excellent choice for developers looking to harness the power of TLS in their applications.

Understanding Rustls ### What is Rustls?

Rustls is a TLS library that emphasizes security and speed while leveraging Rust's memory safety features. It is built with a focus on simplicity and usability, making it an ideal option for developers who want to add TLS capabilities without diving deeply into complex cryptographic details.

Key Features of Rustls

Memory Safety: Rustls embraces Rust's ownership model to ensure memory safety, preventing common issues such as buffer overflows and use-after-free errors.

Modern Protocol Support: Rustls supports the latest versions of TLS (1.2 and 1.3), enabling strong encryption and improved performance.

Simplicity: Rustls comes with straightforward APIs designed for developers of all skill levels, making it easy to integrate TLS into existing applications.

No Dependencies on OpenSSL: Rustls is not dependent on OpenSSL, which reduces the complexity associated with SSL/TLS implementations and potential vulnerabilities.

Setting Up Rustls

To implement TLS in your Rust application using Rustls, you first need to set up your development environment. This involves adding Rustls as a dependency in your Cargo.toml file.

Step 1: Create a new Rust project

```bash
cargo new rustls_example cd rustls_example
```

Step 2: Add Rustls and Required Dependencies

Open your `Cargo.toml` file and add the necessary dependencies:

```toml
[dependencies] rustls = "0.20"
```

tokio = { version = "1", features = ["full"] } tokio-rustls = "0.23"

```
```

Here, we're including `rustls` for TLS functions, `tokio` for asynchronous programming, and `tokio-rustls` for integrating Rustls into the Tokio runtime.

Implementing a Basic TLS Server

Now that we have set up our environment, let's implement a basic TLS server using Rustls. ### Step 1: Generate Self-Signed Certificates

For our example, we'll need TLS certificates. You can create self-signed certificates using the `openssl` command:

```bash
openssl req -newkey rsa:2048 -nodes -keyout key.pem -x509 -days 365 -out cert.pem
```

This command generates a new private key (`key.pem`) and a self-signed certificate (`cert.pem`). ### Step 2: Implement the TLS Server

Create a new file called `main.rs` and implement the TLS server:

```rust
use std::sync::Arc;

use rustls::ServerConfig; use std::fs::File;
```

```rust
use std::io::{BufReader, Error}; use
tokio::net::TcpListener;

use tokio_rustls::{TlsAcceptor, rustls::{ NoClientAuth,
Certificate, PrivateKey }}; use futures::prelude::*;

async fn handle_client(stream:
tokio_rustls::server::TlsStream<tokio::net::TcpStream>)
{
// Handle client connection println!("Client connected!");

// process the stream...
}
#[tokio::main]
async fn main() -> Result<(), Error> {
// Load certificates
let certs = load_certs("cert.pem")?;
let key = load_private_key("key.pem")?;
// Set up TLS configuration
let mut config = ServerConfig::new(NoClientAuth::new());
config.set_single_cert(certs, key).map_err(|_| {
println!("Failed to set certificate and key");
})?;

let acceptor = TlsAcceptor::from(Arc::new(config));

// Bind to address
```

```
let addr = "127.0.0.1:8080";

let listener = TcpListener::bind(addr).await?;
println!("Listening on {}", addr);

loop {

let (socket, _) = listener.accept().await?; let acceptor =
acceptor.clone(); tokio::spawn(async move {

let tls_stream = acceptor.accept(socket).await.unwrap();
handle_client(tls_stream).await;

});

}

}

fn load_certs(filename: &str) -> Result<Vec<Certificate>,
Error> { let certfile = &mut
BufReader::new(File::open(filename)?);
rustls_pemfile::certs(certfile)

.map(|certs| certs.into_iter().map(Certificate).collect())

.map_err(|_| Error::new(std::io::ErrorKind::InvalidData,
"Invalid certificate"))

}

fn load_private_key(filename: &str) ->
Result<PrivateKey, Error> { let keyfile = &mut
BufReader::new(File::open(filename)?);

let keys = rustls_pemfile::keys(keyfile).map_err(|_|
Error::new(std::io::ErrorKind::InvalidData, "Invalid
key"))?;

match keys.get(0) {
```

```
        Some(rustls_pemfile::Item::PKCS8Key(key))        =>
Ok(PrivateKey(key.clone())),

        Some(_)                                          =>
Err(Error::new(std::io::ErrorKind::InvalidData,
"Unsupported      key      format")),      None      =>
Err(Error::new(std::io::ErrorKind::InvalidData, "No keys
found")),
    }
}
```

Explanation:

Loading Certificates: The `load_certs` and `load_private_key` functions handle reading the certificate and private key files, respectively.

TLS Configuration: The `ServerConfig` object initializes with the server's certificate and key. We configure it for no client authentication.

Listening for Connections: The server listens on a specified address and accepts incoming TCP connections.

Handling Clients: A `handle_client` asynchronous function is called when a new connection is established. Here, you can add your logic for handling data exchanges over the TLS-encrypted stream.

Step 3: Running the Server

To run your server, execute the following command:

```bash
cargo run
```

The server should now listen for secure connections on `127.0.0.1:8080`.

In this chapter, we explored implementing TLS using Rustls, a secure, fast, and straightforward TLS library written in Rust. We set up our Rust project, generated self-signed certificates, and created a basic TLS server that securely accepts incoming connections.

With this foundational knowledge, you can now further build on this example to include client authentication, handle TLS sessions more robustly, or create servers that serve specific protocols (e.g., HTTP over TLS).

Encryption and Authentication Techniques

Rust, with its focus on safety and concurrency, offers an excellent platform for implementing secure networked applications. In this chapter, we'll explore key encryption and authentication techniques in Rust and demonstrate how to apply them in network programming contexts.

1. Understanding Encryption

Encryption is the process of converting information into a secure format that hides its actual meaning. It ensures that, even if data is intercepted, it cannot be easily read or understood by unauthorized parties. There are two fundamental types of encryption:

Symmetric Encryption: The same key is used for both encryption and decryption. It's fast and efficient but has key distribution challenges.

Asymmetric Encryption: A pair of keys—public and

private—is used. The public key encrypts the data, and only the private key can decrypt it. While this method is more secure in terms of key distribution, it is slower.

1.1 Encrypting Data with Rust

The `aes` and `rand` crates are commonly used for symmetric encryption, while `rust-openssl` or `ring` can be used for asymmetric encryption. Below is a simple example of using AES for symmetric encryption in Rust:

Setting Up Dependencies

First, add the necessary dependencies to your `Cargo.toml`:

```toml
[dependencies] aes = "0.7.5"
```

block-modes = "0.8.1"

rand = "0.8.4"

```
```

Example: Encrypting and Decrypting Data

```rust
use aes::{Aes128, BlockEncrypt, BlockDecrypt, NewBlockCipher}; use block_modes::{BlockMode, Cbc};
```

use block_modes::Mode;

use rand::{Rng, seq::SliceRandom}; use std::str;

type Aes128Cbc = Cbc<Aes128, block_modes::block_padding::Pkcs7>; fn encrypt(plain_text: &str, key: &[u8; 16]) -> Vec<u8> {

let iv: [u8; 16] = rand::thread_rng().gen();

let cipher = Aes128Cbc::new_from_slices(key,

```rust
&iv).unwrap();          let          mut          buffer          =
plain_text.as_bytes().to_vec();          buffer.resize(16          *
((plain_text.len() + 15) / 16), 0); // Padding let ciphertext
=     cipher.encrypt(&mut     buffer,     iv.len()).unwrap();
[iv.to_vec(), ciphertext.to_vec()].concat()
}

fn   decrypt(cipher_text:   &[u8],   key:   &[u8;   16])   ->
Option<String> { let (iv, data) = cipher_text.split_at(16);

let     cipher     =     Aes128Cbc::new_from_slices(key,
iv).unwrap(); let mut buffer = data.to_vec();

if          cipher.decrypt(&mut          buffer).is_ok()          {
Some(String::from_utf8_lossy(&buffer).to_string())

} else {

None

}

}

fn main() {

let key: [u8; 16] = *b"an_example_key_";

let plain_text = "Secure Data";

let     cipher_text     =     encrypt(plain_text,     &key);
println!("Encrypted: {:?}", cipher_text);

if let Some(decrypted) = decrypt(&cipher_text, &key) {
println!("Decrypted: {}", decrypted);

} else {

println!("Decryption failed");

}
```

```
}
```

2. Authentication Techniques

Authentication is the process of verifying the identity of a user or system. It's critical for ensuring that only authorized users can access resources. Common techniques include:

Password-based Authentication: Users provide a username and password, which are validated against stored values.

Token-based Authentication: Users log in once and are issued a token, which they use for subsequent requests.

Public-Key Infrastructure (PKI): Uses digital certificates to verify identity. ### 2.1 Implementing Token-Based Authentication

In many modern applications, token-based authentication is preferred due to its stateless nature and scalability. Below is an example of JWT (JSON Web Token) creation using `jsonwebtoken`:

Setting Up Dependencies

```toml [dependencies]
jsonwebtoken = "8.1.0"
```

Example: Issuing and Validating a JWT

```rust
```

```rust
use jsonwebtoken::{encode, decode, Header, Algorithm,
Validation, EncodingKey, DecodingKey}; use
serde::{Serialize, Deserialize};

#[derive(Debug, Serialize, Deserialize)] struct Claims {

sub: String, exp: usize,

}

fn create_jwt(user_id: &str, secret: &[u8]) -> String { let
claims = Claims {

sub: user_id.to_string(),

exp: 10000000000, // should be a proper expiration time

};

encode(&Header::default(),                        &claims,
&EncodingKey::from_secret(secret)).unwrap()

}

fn validate_jwt(token:    &str,    secret:    &[u8])    ->
Result<Claims,        jsonwebtoken::errors::Error>        {
decode::<Claims>(token,
&DecodingKey::from_secret(secret),
&Validation::default())

.map(|data| data.claims)

}

fn main() {

let secret = b"your_secret_key";

let jwt = create_jwt("user123", secret); println!("JWT: {}",
jwt);

match validate_jwt(&jwt, secret) {
```

```
Ok(claims) => println!("Claims: {:?}", claims),
Err(e) => println!("Invalid token: {}", e),
}
}
```

3. Combining Encryption and Authentication

In practice, employing both encryption and authentication together is essential for securing communications. For example, you can encrypt sensitive data before sending it over the network, and use JWT or another authentication method to ensure that the requests are made by verified users.

By leveraging libraries like `aes`, `jsonwebtoken`, and others, developers can create secure applications that protect sensitive data and verify user identities. As you continue to build scalable and secure networked solutions, understanding and applying these techniques will be crucial in ensuring safety and privacy in your applications.

Chapter 8: Building RESTful APIs with Rust

Rust, known for its speed, safety, and concurrency capabilities, is an excellent choice for building high-performance networked applications, including RESTful APIs.

What is REST?

Representational State Transfer (REST) is an architectural style that utilizes HTTP requests to create, read, update, and delete data. The core principles of REST include statelessness, client-server separation, uniform interfaces, and resource-based operations. By adhering to these principles, developers can create scalable and maintainable web services.

Why Rust?

Rust brings unique advantages to the table:

Performance: Rust's compilation to Machine Code makes it a suitable option for high-performance applications.

Memory Safety: Rust's strict ownership model prevents various memory-related issues such as null pointer dereferences, data races, and buffer overflows.

Concurrency: Rust provides powerful abstractions for safe concurrent programming, allowing developers to write highly concurrent applications without encountering typical pitfalls.

In this chapter, we will walk through the steps of building a simple RESTful API using Rust, focusing on the Axum framework, which is designed to make building APIs in Rust seamless and secure.

Getting Started with Axum   ### Setting Up Your Environment

To start building your RESTful API with Rust, you need to ensure you have Rust installed. If not, you can follow these steps:

Install Rust using `rustup`:

```bash
curl --proto '=https' --tlsv1.2 -sSf https://sh.rustup.rs | sh
```

Create a new project:

```bash
cargo new rust_rest_api cd rust_rest_api
```

Adding Dependencies

Now, let's add Axum along with some essential libraries to our `Cargo.toml`:

```toml [dependencies]
```

```
axum = "0.6"

tokio = { version = "1", features = ["full"] } serde = {
version = "1", features = ["derive"] } serde_json = "1.0"
```
```

### Creating a Simple API

Let's create a simple RESTful API that manages a
collection of books. We will define our `Book` struct,
which will represent the book entity.

```rust
use        axum::{        extract::{Path,        Json},
response::IntoResponse, routing::{get, post}, Router,

};

use serde::{Deserialize, Serialize}; use std::{sync::Arc,
sync::Mutex};

#[derive(Serialize, Deserialize, Clone)] struct Book {

id: usize, title: String,

author: String,

}

type      Database      =      Arc<Mutex<Vec<Book>>>;
#[tokio::main]

async fn main() {

let db = Arc::new(Mutex::new(Vec::new()));


let app = Router::new()

.route("/books", get(get_books).post(create_book))
```
```

```
.layer(axum::AddExtensionLayer::new(db));
axum::Server::bind(&"0.0.0.0:3000".parse().unwrap())
.serve(app.into_make_service())
.await
.unwrap();
}
```

In this code snippet, we define the `Book` struct and use `Arc` and `Mutex` to wrap our in-memory database, allowing safe concurrent access from multiple threads. The main function initializes the server, setting it to listen on port 3000.

Implementing Handlers

Let's implement the handlers for getting and creating books:

```rust
async fn get_books(db: axum::extract::Extension<Database>) -> impl IntoResponse { let db = db.lock().unwrap();

Json(db.clone())
}
async fn create_book(

axum::extract::Json(new_book): axum::extract::Json<Book>, db: axum::extract::Extension<Database>
) -> impl IntoResponse {
```

```
let mut db = db.lock().unwrap(); let book_id = db.len() +
1;

let book = Book { id: book_id, title: new_book.title,
author: new_book.author };

db.push(book);        (axum::http::StatusCode::CREATED,
Json(book))

}
```

The `get_books` handler retrieves the collection of books,
while the `create_book` handler adds a new book to the
database. Both handlers utilize the `Json` extractor from
Axum to handle JSON payloads easily.

Testing the API

With our API in place, you can test it using a tool such as
`curl` or Postman. To retrieve books, you can use:

```bash
curl http://localhost:3000/books
```

To create a new book, you can send a POST request:

```bash
curl -X POST http://localhost:3000/books -H "Content-
Type: application/json" -d '{"title": "1984", "author":
"George Orwell"}'
```

Error Handling

When developing RESTful APIs, robust error handling is

128

vital. Axum allows you to define custom error types and easily return meaningful error messages. Consider creating an error handler that returns appropriate HTTP status codes and messages.

```rust
use axum::{ Error,

http::StatusCode, response::{IntoResponse, Response}

};

async fn handle_error(error: Error) -> (StatusCode, String) { (StatusCode::INTERNAL_SERVER_ERROR, error.to_string())

}
```

To use this error handler, you would need to modify your routes accordingly. This will ensure that your API responds appropriately to errors, maintaining the client experience.

Building RESTful APIs with Rust using the Axum framework proves to be both straightforward and efficient. Throughout this chapter, we discovered how to set up our environment, create a simple book management API, and implement basic error handling.

Using Actix-Web for API Development

One of the shining stars in the Rust ecosystem is Actix-Web, a powerful framework for building web applications and APIs. This chapter explores how to leverage Actix-Web for API development, showcasing its features, benefits, and best practices, all within the context of network programming.

Why Choose Rust and Actix-Web?

Before diving into the specifics of Actix-Web, it's important to understand why Rust and this framework are excellent choices for network programming:

Memory Safety: Rust's ownership model prevents common bugs like null pointer dereferences and data races. This is critical when building network applications where stability and reliability are paramount.

Performance: Rust compiles to native code, ensuring high performance. Actix-Web is designed to be fast, making it suitable for handling many connections simultaneously.

Concurrency: Rust provides powerful abstractions for concurrency without sacrificing safety. Actix- Web takes advantage of this, allowing developers to build highly concurrent server applications.

Rich Ecosystem: Rust's ecosystem is continuously growing, with a vibrant community and libraries that support various functionalities needed in API development.

Getting Started with Actix-Web ### Setting Up Your Environment

To begin using Actix-Web, make sure you have Rust and Cargo installed. If not, you can download them from the [official Rust website](https://www.rust-lang.org/tools/install).

Once Rust is set up, create a new project using Cargo:

```bash
cargo new actix_web_api cd actix_web_api
```

Next, you need to add Actix-Web as a dependency. Open `Cargo.toml` and add the following lines under `[dependencies]`:

```toml
[dependencies]
actix-web = "4.0"  # Choose the latest version
```

Building a Simple API

Let's build a basic REST API that handles a simple resource: "messages." We will create endpoints to create, read, update, and delete messages.

Step 1: Define the Message Structure

First, create a new file, `model.rs`, to define our `Message` strut.

```rust
// model.rs
use serde::{Serialize, Deserialize};

#[derive(Debug, Serialize, Deserialize)] pub struct Message {
id: usize, content: String,
}
```

```
```

Step 2: Implement the API Handlers

Next, we'll implement the API handlers in `main.rs`:

```rust
// main.rs

use actix_web::{post, get, delete, web, App, HttpServer, HttpResponse}; use std::sync::Mutex;

use std::collections::HashMap;

mod model;

use model::Message;

struct AppState {

messages: Mutex<HashMap<usize, Message>>,

}

#[post("/messages")]

async fn create_message(state: web::Data<AppState>, msg: web::Json<Message>) -> HttpResponse { let mut messages = state.messages.lock().unwrap();

let id = messages.len() + 1; let message = Message {

id,

content: msg.content.clone(),

};

messages.insert(id,                                      message); HttpResponse::Created().json(message)

}
```

```rust
#[get("/messages/{id}")]
async fn get_message(state: web::Data<AppState>, id: web::Path<usize>) -> HttpResponse { let messages = state.messages.lock().unwrap();

if let Some(message) = messages.get(&id.into_inner()) {
HttpResponse::Ok().json(message)

} else {

HttpResponse::NotFound().finish()

}

}

#[delete("/messages/{id}")]
async fn delete_message(state: web::Data<AppState>, id: web::Path<usize>) -> HttpResponse {


let mut messages = state.messages.lock().unwrap(); if messages.remove(&id.into_inner()).is_some() {

HttpResponse::Ok().finish()

} else {

HttpResponse::NotFound().finish()

}

}

#[actix_web::main]

async fn main() -> std::io::Result<()> {

let app_state = web::Data::new(AppState { messages: Mutex::new(HashMap::new()),
```

```
});
HttpServer::new(move || { App::new()
.app_data(app_state.clone())
.service(create_message)
.service(get_message)
.service(delete_message)
})
.bind("127.0.0.1:8080")?
.run()
.await
}
```

Step 3: Running the Server

You can now run the server with the command:

```bash
cargo run
```

The server will be accessible at `http://127.0.0.1:8080`. You can use tools like `curl` or Postman to test your API:

- **Create a message**:

```bash
curl -X POST -H "Content-Type: application/json" -d '{"content": "Hello, World!"}' http://127.0.0.1:8080/messages
```

- **Get a message by ID**:
```bash
curl http://127.0.0.1:8080/messages/1
```

- **Delete a message**:
```bash
curl -X DELETE http://127.0.0.1:8080/messages/1
```

Best Practices in Actix-Web

While building APIs with Actix-Web, consider the following best practices:

Error Handling: Implement proper error handling using the `Result` type and HTTP responses to reliably communicate errors to clients.

Asynchronous Programming: Utilize Rust's async capabilities for non-blocking I/O operations, making your application more scalable.

Testing: Leverage Actix-Web's built-in testing tools to write unit and integration tests for your API endpoints.

Security: Apply security best practices, such as input validation, rate limiting, and using HTTPS for data in transit.

Logging: Integrate logging to monitor your API's behavior, making debugging and performance analysis easier.

Rust provides a solid foundation for creating high-performance and safe network applications, and with Actix-Web, developers can take full advantage of these features to deliver robust APIs.

Securing Your APIs with Middleware

We will cover concepts, practical implementations, and security best practices that can help you refine your network programming skills while building secure applications.

5.1 Understanding Middleware

Middleware serves as a bridge between different applications or services and handles various functions such as routing, authentication, logging, and error handling. In the context of web APIs, middleware plays a crucial role in processing requests and responses, allowing developers to separate concerns and apply security measures universally across multiple routes or endpoints.

5.1.1 Types of Middleware

Middleware can take various forms, serving different purposes:

Authentication Middleware: Verifies user credentials and manages session tokens.

Logging Middleware: Captures request and response data for debugging and audit purposes.

Error Handling Middleware: Catches errors that occur during request processing and formats responses appropriately.

Rate Limiting Middleware: Controls the number of requests a user can make in a specified time frame.

CORS Middleware: Manages Cross-Origin Resource Sharing policies to restrict access to resources. ## 5.2 Setting Up a Rust Web Framework

To implement middleware in Rust, we will use a popular web framework, **Actix-web**. This framework is lightweight, powerful, and provides excellent support for middleware development.

5.2.1 Creating a New Project

To get started, ensure you have Rust and Cargo installed. Create a new Actix-web project by running:

```bash

cargo new rust_api_security cd rust_api_security
```

Next, add Actix-web to your `Cargo.toml`:

```toml [dependencies] actix-web = "4.0"
```

5.2.2 Basic Server Setup

Let's start by setting up a basic HTTP server:

```rust

use actix_web::{web, App, HttpServer, Responder};
```

```rust
async fn index() -> impl Responder { "Hello, world!"
}
#[actix_web::main]
async fn main() -> std::io::Result<()> {
HttpServer::new(|| {
App::new()
.route("/", web::get().to(index))
})
.bind("127.0.0.1:8080")?
.run()
.await
}
```

To run the server, execute `cargo run`, and you should see "Hello, world!" when visiting

`http://localhost:8080`.

5.3 Implementing Middleware

Now that we have a basic server, let's implement a middleware that adds a security layer over our API. ### 5.3.1 Authentication Middleware

Here's how you can create an authentication middleware that checks if an API key is present in the headers:

```rust
use actix_web::{dev::Service, web, App, HttpRequest, HttpServer, Responder, Result}; use
```

```
actix_service::ServiceExt;

async fn authenticate(req: HttpRequest) -> Result<impl
Responder>    {    if    let    Some(api_key)    =
req.headers().get("X-API-KEY") {

if api_key == "my_secret_api_key" { // Replace with an
appropriate check return Ok("API key is valid");

}

}

Err(actix_web::error::ErrorUnauthorized("Unauthorized")
)

}

#[actix_web::main]

async    fn    main()    ->    std::io::Result<()>    {
HttpServer::new(|| {

App::new()

.wrap_fn(|req, next| {

let headers = req.headers().clone(); async move {

if    let    Ok(response)    =    authenticate(req).await    {
next.call(req).await

} else {

Err(actix_web::error::ErrorUnauthorized("Unauthorized")
)

}

}

}

})
```

```rust
    .route("/", web::get().to(index))
})
.bind("127.0.0.1:8080")?
.run()
.await
}
```

In this example, we create a custom middleware function, `authenticate`, that checks the existence of an API key in the headers. If the API key is missing or invalid, the server responds with a "401 Unauthorized" status.

5.3.2 Error Handling Middleware

Adding robust error handling to our API is equally important. We can implement a basic error middleware as follows:

```rust
async fn error_handler<B>(res: actix_web::dev::ServiceResponse<B>) -> actix_web::dev::ServiceResponse<B> {

if res.status().is_client_error() {

println!("Client error occurred: {}", res.status());

}


if res.status().is_server_error() {

println!("Server error occurred: {}", res.status());
```

```
}

res
}
HttpServer::new(|| { App::new()
.wrap_fn(|req, next| {
let        response        =        next.call(req).await;
error_handler(response).await
})
.route("/", web::get().to(index))
})
```
```

The `error_handler` function processes the response and logs any client or server errors that occur, allowing you to monitor and respond to issues effectively.

## 5.4 Security Best Practices

While the middleware we have implemented provides a layer of security, consider adopting the following best practices to enhance the security of your Rust APIs:

**Use HTTPS**: Always serve your API over HTTPS to encrypt traffic between the client and server.

**Validate Inputs**: Implement input validation to prevent injection attacks and other malicious inputs.

**Utilize Rate Limiting**: Protect your API from abuse by limiting the rate of requests a client can make.

**Implement CORS Carefully**: Configure Cross-Origin
```

Resource Sharing (CORS) to only allow trusted domains.

Keep Dependencies Updated: Regularly update your dependencies to incorporate the latest security patches.

By understanding the types of middleware and implementing basic authentication and error handling, you can lay the groundwork for creating secure and reliable applications. As you continue developing your APIs, always remain vigilant about new security risks and updates in best practices to protect your users and your data effectively.

Chapter 9: Real-Time Communication with WebSockets

This chapter will explore how to leverage Rust, a systems programming language known for its performance and reliability, to implement WebSocket communication in network applications.

9.1 Understanding WebSockets

WebSocket is a protocol that provides full-duplex communication channels over a single TCP connection. It is especially advantageous for applications that require real-time updates, such as chat applications, live notifications, and online gaming.

Key Features of WebSockets

Full-Duplex Communication: Both the client and server can send and receive messages independently without having to wait for the other to finish.

Reduced Latency: Once the connection is established, data can flow freely in both directions, minimizing the overhead of repeated requests and responses.

Persistent Connection: Unlike traditional HTTP, which opens a new connection for each request, WebSockets maintain a persistent connection, allowing for better resource utilization.

9.2 Setting Up a Rust Environment

Before diving into WebSocket programming in Rust, we need to set up our development environment. Ensure you have Rust installed on your system. If not, you can install it using `rustup`, the official installer for Rust.

```bash
curl --proto '=https' --tlsv1.2 -sSf https://sh.rustup.rs | sh
```

After installation, create a new Rust project:

```bash
cargo new websocket_example cd websocket_example
```

In the `Cargo.toml` file, include the necessary dependencies for WebSocket support. One popular choice is the `tokio-tungstenite` library, which combines the `tungstenite` WebSocket library with `tokio`, an asynchronous runtime for Rust.

```toml
[dependencies]
tokio = { version = "1", features = ["full"] } tungstenite = "0.15"

tokio-tungstenite = "0.15"
```

9.3 Creating a WebSocket Server

With our environment set up, let's start building a simple WebSocket server that echoes messages back to clients.

Step 1: Importing Necessary Libraries

In the `src/main.rs`, we start by importing the required libraries:

```rust
```

```rust
use tokio::net::TcpListener;
use tokio_tungstenite::accept_async; use futures_util::{SinkExt, StreamExt}; use std::error::Error;
```

Step 2: Implementing the WebSocket Server

Next, we define our main asynchronous function where the WebSocket server will be set up. The server will listen for incoming connections and handle them asynchronously.

```rust
#[tokio::main]
async fn main() -> Result<(), Box<dyn Error>> { let addr = "127.0.0.1:8080";

let listener = TcpListener::bind(&addr).await?; println!("WebSocket server listening on {}", addr);

while let Ok((stream, _)) = listener.accept().await {

let ws_stream = accept_async(stream).await.expect("Error during WebSocket handshake"); println!("New WebSocket connection established");

tokio::spawn(handle_connection(ws_stream));

}

Ok(())

}
```

Step 3: Handling WebSocket Connections

Now we need to implement the `handle_connection`

145

function that reads messages from the client and echoes them back.

```rust
async fn handle_connection(ws_stream: tokio_tungstenite::WebSocketStream<tokio::net::TcpStream>) { let (mut write, mut read) = ws_stream.split();

while let Some(msg) = read.next().await { match msg {

Ok(message) => {

if write.send(message).await.is_err() { eprintln!("Error sending message"); return;

}
}


Err(e) => {

eprintln!("Error reading message: {}", e); return;

}
}
}
}
```

9.4 Creating a WebSocket Client

Now that our server is ready, we can create a simple WebSocket client to test our implementation. A client can connect to the server and send messages.

Step 1: Client Setup

Create a new Rust binary project for the client:

```bash
cargo new websocket_client cd websocket_client
```

Edit the `Cargo.toml` to include necessary dependencies:

```toml
[dependencies]
tokio = { version = "1", features = ["full"] } tokio-tungstenite = "0.15"
futures-util = "0.3"
```

Step 2: Implementing the WebSocket Client

In the `src/main.rs` of the client project, connect to the WebSocket server and send a message.

```rust
use                    tokio_tungstenite::{connect_async,
tungstenite::protocol::Message};                   use
futures_util::stream::StreamExt;

#[tokio::main] async fn main() {

let url = "ws://127.0.0.1:8080";

let            (ws_stream,            _)            =
connect_async(url).await.expect("Failed  to  connect");
println!("Connected to WebSocket server");

let (mut write, mut read) = ws_stream.split();

write.send(Message::Text("Hello,
WebSocket!".into())).await.expect("Failed    to    send
message");
```

147

```rust
while let Some(msg) = read.next().await { match msg {
Ok(message) => {
println!("Received: {:?}", message);
}
Err(e) => { eprintln!("Error: {}", e);
}
}
}
}
```

9.5 Testing the Application

To test the WebSocket server and client, first run the server:

```bash
cargo run
```

In another terminal window, run the client:

```bash
cargo run
```

Once the client sends a message, the server should echo it back, and both should print the relevant logs to the console.

This powerful duo enables building responsive applications where users can interact dynamically with real- time data. As you continue your journey with Rust and network programming, consider experimenting further with authentication, message broadcasting, and integrating libraries like `serde` for structured data handling.

Creating WebSocket Clients and Servers

In this chapter, we'll explore how to create a WebSocket client and server in Rust using the `tokio` ecosystem, which allows for asynchronous programming and efficient resource management.

Setting Up the Rust Environment

Before diving into coding, ensure that you have Rust installed on your system. You can download it from [rust-lang.org](https://www.rust-lang.org/). Once installed, you can check the installation by running:

```bash
rustc --version
```

Creating a New Project

To create a new Rust project, use Cargo, Rust's package manager:

```bash
cargo new websocket_example cd websocket_example
```

This command creates a new directory with a basic Rust project structure. You will modify the `Cargo.toml` file to add the necessary dependencies for WebSocket support.

Adding Dependencies

Open the `Cargo.toml` file and add the following dependencies:

```toml [dependencies]
tokio = { version = "1", features = ["full"] } tokio-tungstenite = "0.17"

tungstenite = "0.18"
```

`tokio` is an asynchronous runtime for Rust.

`tokio-tungstenite` allows the use of WebSockets in a `tokio` environment.

`tungstenite` is a WebSocket library for Rust.

Now that we have our setup, it's time to implement a WebSocket server. ## Implementing a WebSocket Server

Step 1: Setting Up the Server

Create a new file named `server.rs` in the `src` directory and add the following code:

```rust
use tokio::net::TcpListener;

use tokio_tungstenite::tungstenite::{accept, Error};


use tokio_tungstenite::accept_async;     use futures_util::stream::StreamExt;     use futures_util::SinkExt;
```

```rust
#[tokio::main] async fn main() {

let addr = "127.0.0.1:8080";

let listener = TcpListener::bind(&addr).await.unwrap();
println!("WebSocket server is running on: {}", addr);

while let Ok((stream, _)) = listener.accept().await {
tokio::spawn(handle_connection(stream));

}

}

async fn handle_connection(stream:
tokio::net::TcpStream) { let ws_stream =
accept_async(stream)

.await

.expect("Error during WebSocket handshake");
println!("New client connected!");

let (mut ws_sender, mut ws_receiver) =
ws_stream.split();

while let Some(message) = ws_receiver.next().await {
match message {

Ok(msg) => {

println!("Received a message: {:?}", msg);

// Echo the message back to the client
ws_sender.send(msg).await.expect("Failed to send a
message");

},

Err(e) => {

eprintln!("Error while receiving message: {}", e); return;
```

```
        }
    }
    }
}
```

Explanation

Imports: The code imports necessary components from `tokio`, `tokio_tungstenite`, and

`futures_util`.

Main Function: The main function initializes a TCP listener on localhost at port 8080. It listens for incoming connections and spawns a new task for each connection.

Handling Connections: The `handle_connection` function handles each connection. It performs the WebSocket handshake and splits the stream into a sender and receiver. Messages received from clients are printed and echoed back.

Step 2: Running the Server

To run the WebSocket server, execute the following command in your terminal:

```bash
cargo run --bin server
```

You should see an output indicating that the server is running and ready to accept connections. ##

Implementing a WebSocket Client

Step 1: Creating the Client

Now let's create a simple WebSocket client. Create a new file named `client.rs` in the `src` directory. Add the following code to `client.rs`:

```rust
use tokio_tungstenite::connect_async;

use tokio_tungstenite::tungstenite::protocol::Message;

#[tokio::main] async fn main() {

let url = "ws://127.0.0.1:8080";

let (ws_stream, _) = connect_async(url).await.expect("Failed to connect"); let (mut ws_sender, mut ws_receiver) = ws_stream.split();

// Send a message to the server

ws_sender.send(Message::Text("Hello, WebSocket!".into())).await.expect("Failed to send message");

// Receive messages

while let Some(message) = ws_receiver.next().await { match message {

Ok(msg) => println!("Received from server: {:?}", msg),
Err(e) => eprintln!("WebSocket error: {}", e),

}

}

}
```

Explanation

Connecting: The client connects to the running WebSocket server using `connect_async`.

Sending a Message: After establishing a connection, the client sends a message "Hello, WebSocket!" to the server.

Receiving Messages: It listens for messages coming back from the server and prints them. ### Step 2: Running the Client

In a new terminal window, run the WebSocket client with:

```bash
cargo run --bin client
```

You should see the client send a message and receive an echo response from the server.

Using the `tokio` and `tokio-tungstenite` libraries simplifies the process of handling asynchronous WebSocket communication, allowing you to build responsive and efficient real-time applications.

Use Cases for Real-Time Applications

As the demand for high-performance, reliable, and efficient network applications grows, Rust has emerged as a language of choice for building real-time systems. Combining safety, concurrency, and performance, Rust offers developers the tools they need to create robust network applications that can handle real-time data streams. This chapter explores various use cases for real-time applications that leverage Rust's strengths in network programming.

1. Real-Time Communication Protocols

One of the primary use cases for Rust in network programming is the development of real-time communication protocols. With the rise of applications that require low-latency interactions—such as VoIP, video conferencing, and collaborative tools—there is an increasing demand for efficient and reliable networking libraries.

Example: WebRTC Implementation

WebRTC (Web Real-Time Communication) enables peer-to-peer communication between browsers and mobile applications. Rust can be used to implement WebRTC clients or servers that facilitate real-time audio and video streaming. Rust's ownership model ensures memory safety, which is critical for applications that handle sensitive data, reducing the risk of vulnerabilities such as buffer overflows.

Advantages:

Performance: Rust's ability to deliver high performance through zero-cost abstractions makes it suitable for applications needing real-time capabilities.

Safety: The compile-time checks help eliminate common programming errors, thus ensuring a stable communication layer.

2. Streaming Data Processing

Data streaming applications are critical in industries such as finance, telecommunications, and online content delivery. Rust's concurrency model allows developers to build scalable streaming platforms that process data in real time while maintaining low latency.

Example: Real-Time Analytics Engine

Imagine a financial application that analyzes stock market data in real time, providing users with actionable insights. Rust can be harnessed to develop an analytics engine that processes incoming data streams, performs statistical calculations, and sends alerts to users.

Advantages:

Concurrency: With Rust's powerful concurrency primitives, developers can efficiently manage multiple streams of data without running into race conditions.

Interoperability: Rust's ability to interface with C and other languages allows for integration with existing data processing libraries, facilitating a smoother transition for teams considering Rust for their stack.

3. Game Development and Multiplayer Gaming

The gaming industry has increasingly adopted Rust for developing real-time multiplayer games. The low latency and high reliability of Rust make it an excellent candidate for game servers and real-time gaming experiences.

Example: Real-Time Strategy Game Server

Developing a real-time strategy (RTS) game requires a game server that can handle numerous players simultaneously, synchronize game states, and manage real-time interactions. Rust can be utilized to build a backend server that ensures low-latency communication between players and the game world.

Advantages:

Memory Efficiency: Rust's ownership system can help manage game state data more efficiently, reducing memory overhead associated with traditional game engines.

Parallelism: The ability to perform parallel computations can lead to improved game performance, particularly in simulations involving multiple entities interacting in real time.

4. Internet of Things (IoT)

The IoT space is rapidly expanding, with billions of devices generating and communicating massive amounts of data. Rust's memory safety features, combined with its minimal runtime and performance efficiency, make it ideal for IoT applications that require real-time data processing.

Example: Smart Home Device Management

Consider an IoT platform that manages smart home devices. Using Rust, developers can create a controller that communicates with multiple devices, processes incoming data from sensors, and responds to user commands in real time.

Advantages:

Low Resource Footprint: Rust's efficiency allows for the development of applications that can run on devices with limited processing capabilities.

Safety and Security: With the pervasive concern about

security in IoT, Rust's strong emphasis on safety helps mitigate vulnerabilities often exploited in less secure languages.

5. Financial Trading Systems

In the financial sector, trading systems require real-time data processing, analysis, and transaction execution. Rust's performance characteristics make it an attractive option for building such systems where milliseconds can mean significant monetary gain or loss.

Example: High-Frequency Trading (HFT) Software

High-frequency trading relies on executing a large number of orders at extremely high speeds. A trading application built in Rust can take advantage of zero-cost abstractions and low-level control over system resources to optimize performance.

Advantages:

Deterministic Performance: Rust enables developers to write code with predictable performance, which is vital in high-stakes environments like trading.

Concurrency: The language's concurrency features make it possible to handle many simultaneous transactions efficiently without sacrificing safety.

The use cases discussed in this chapter illustrate how Rust is shaping the future of network programming, paving the way for innovations in various industries. As the ecosystem continues to grow, more developers are likely to explore Rust for their real-time application needs, ultimately redefining the landscape of network programming.

Chapter 10: Testing and Debugging Network Applications

This chapter explores techniques and best practices for effectively testing and debugging network applications written in Rust.

10.1 Introduction to Testing in Rust

Rust features built-in support for unit testing and integration testing. The `cargo test` command facilitates running tests, making it easy to set up a testing environment. The primary goal of testing network applications is to ensure that they behave as expected under various conditions and that edge cases are handled gracefully.

10.1.1 Unit Tests

Unit tests are designed to test small pieces of functionality in isolation. In the context of network applications, unit tests can focus on individual functions, error handling, and data manipulation.

Example:

```rust
#[cfg(test)] mod tests {

use super::*;

#[test]

fn test_example_function() { let input = "test input";

let expected_output = "expected output";
assert_eq!(example_function(input), expected_output);

}
}
```

```
```

Utilizing mocks and stubs can help isolate units of code to verify their correctness without relying on external network calls.

10.1.2 Integration Tests

Integration tests evaluate how various components interact. In network applications, you might wish to test the interaction between a server and a client or ensure the proper functionality of an API endpoint.

Creating an integration test involves placing a file in the `tests` directory of your project. Example:

```rust #[test]
fn test_api_endpoint() {

let                        response                      =
reqwest::blocking::get("http://localhost:8000/api/test")

.expect("Failed to get response");

assert_eq!(response.status(), 200);

}
```

By using test frameworks like `reqwest` for making HTTP requests, you can simulate real-world network interactions.

10.2 Error Handling in Network Applications

When building network applications, handling errors gracefully is essential. Rust's `Result` and `Option` types are vital for expressing outcomes in a way that compels developers to deal with potential errors.

Example:

```rust
fn perform_request(url: &str) -> Result<String, Box<dyn Error>> { let response = reqwest::blocking::get(url)?;

let body = response.text()?; Ok(body)

}
```

Implementing thorough error handling increases the reliability of your application. Ensure that all potential failure points are accounted for, and provide meaningful error messages to help diagnose issues.

10.3 Writing Tests for Concurrency

Network applications often employ concurrent programming models, making testing more complex. Rust's ownership model and types like `Arc` and `Mutex` simplify safe concurrency. However, they also introduce challenges in verification.

To test concurrent code, you can use the `tokio` runtime for asynchronous testing. Combine this with Rust's threading capabilities to make assertions about the state of your application under concurrent load.

Example:

```rust #[tokio::test]
async fn test_concurrent_requests() { let handle1 = tokio::spawn(async {

// Simulate a request

});
```

```rust
let handle2 = tokio::spawn(async {
// Simulate another request
});
let res1 = handle1.await.unwrap(); let res2 = handle2.await.unwrap();
// Assert results from both concurrent requests
}
```

10.4 Using Test Doubles

In integration tests, you may want to avoid hitting real network endpoints for stability and speed reasons. Test doubles like mocks and fakes can simulate parts of your application during testing.

You can use libraries such as `mockito` to create mock servers and simulate responses to your network requests:

```rust
#[macro_use]
extern crate mockito;
#[test]
fn test_mock_api() {
let _m = mockito::mock("GET", "/api/test")
.with_status(200)
.with_body("mocked response")
.create();
let                    response                    =
```

```rust
reqwest::blocking::get(&format!("{}/api/test",
mockito::server_url()))
.expect("Request failed");

assert_eq!(response.text().unwrap(), "mocked response");
}
```

This approach allows you to focus tests on the logical flow of your network application without being hindered by actual network availability or reliability.

10.5 Debugging Techniques

Debugging is an art in software development; it becomes a bit more nuanced in the context of network applications due to the complexities of asynchronous programming and concurrency.

10.5.1 Logging

Effective logging is your first step towards easy debugging. Use the `log` and `env_logger` crates to incorporate logging at various levels. This enables you to record actions, errors, and flow of execution throughout your application.

Example:

```rust
fn main() { env_logger::init();

log::info!("Starting the server...");
}
```

```

```

With logging, inspect your application's behavior in real time, which can be instrumental when diagnosing issues that arise in production.

10.5.2 Debugging Tools

Utilize tools like `gdb`, Rust's integrated debugger, as well as the built-in `cargo expand` command to view expanded macros and help trace issues. Additionally, IDEs like Visual Studio Code and IntelliJ Rust can streamline debugging processes with their user-friendly interfaces.

10.5.3 Error Analysis

When a network error occurs, provide informative outputs that describe not just the error, but the state that led to it. This helps to trace problems back to their source, making debugging much clearer.

Example of an error output:

```rust
err_log!("Failed to connect to server at {}: {:?}", address, e);
```

Testing and debugging network applications in Rust can be simplified through effective use of Rust's ecosystem features such as structured error handling, robust testing frameworks, and effective logging practices. By employing these techniques, developers can ensure the reliability of their network applications and create a solid foundation for user trust.

Writing Unit and Integration Tests for Networking Code

Networking code is inherently complex, often involving various protocols, concurrency, and external resources. When developing networking applications in Rust, it is crucial to ensure that your code performs correctly under various conditions. This chapter will guide you through writing unit and integration tests for your networking code, ensuring robustness and reliability.

Understanding Testing in Rust

Rust has a built-in testing framework that supports both unit and integration tests. Unit tests are written in the same file as the code they are testing, while integration tests reside in a separate directory. This structure promotes organization and clarity in your test suite.

Unit Tests

Unit tests verify individual components of your application, focusing on small pieces of functionality. For networking code, unit tests could include checks for correct input processing, error handling, and response validation.

Structure of Unit Tests

Rust unit tests are typically defined in a `#[cfg(test)]` module within the source file. Here's an example of how to write unit tests for a simple networking function in Rust.

```rust
// src/lib.rs

pub fn parse_url(url: &str) -> Result<(String, u16),
```

```rust
String> { let mut parts = url.split(':');

let hostname = parts.next().ok_or("Invalid
URL")?.to_string(); let port = parts.next().ok_or("Invalid
URL")?.parse::<u16>()

.map_err(|_| "Invalid port number")?;

Ok((hostname, port))
}
#[cfg(test)] mod tests {
use super::*;
#[test]
fn test_parse_url_valid() {
assert_eq!(parse_url("example.com:8080").unwrap(),
("example.com".to_string(), 8080));
}
#[test]
fn              test_parse_url_no_port()              {
assert!(parse_url("example.com").is_err());
}


#[test]
fn              test_parse_url_invalid_port()              {
assert!(parse_url("example.com:invalid").is_err());
}
}
```
```
```

In the example above, we have a simple function `parse_url` that separates a hostname from a port number. The unit tests validate its behavior under expected and erroneous conditions. By using `assert_eq!` and

`assert!`, we can verify that our function behaves as intended. ### Integration Tests

While unit tests focus on individual functions, integration tests check how components work together. Integration tests can be particularly helpful in networking code when testing how various services communicate or how your application behaves in a real-world environment.

Structure of Integration Tests

Integration tests are placed in the `tests` directory, which is a sibling to your `src` directory. Each file in this directory is compiled as a separate crate, allowing you to test your code without the internal knowledge of your module.

```rust
// tests/integration_test.rs

use my_networking_lib::parse_url; #[test]

fn test_parse_valid_url_integration() {

let result = parse_url("myapp.local:3000"); assert!(result.is_ok());


let (hostname, port) = result.unwrap(); assert_eq!(hostname, "myapp.local"); assert_eq!(port, 3000);
```

```
}
#[test]
fn test_parse_url_with_invalid_format() {
let result = parse_url("myapp.local:three-thousand");
assert!(result.is_err());
}
#[test]
fn test_service_interaction() {
// Simulating interaction with an external URL
// This could involve mocking or stubbing a service.
// For real network interactions, ensure your code can handle
// various states and responses. use crate::mock_service;
let response = mock_service::get("http://example.com/resource");
assert_eq!(response.status(), 200);


}
```
```

The integration tests in this example check the `parse_url` function while also demonstrating how to start testing service interactions. When testing networking functionalities, consider simulating service responses or using mocking libraries.

### Mocking Network Interactions

Testing real network interactions can be unpredictable
```

and slow. Utilizing mocking libraries allows you to simulate network services without making actual network requests. One commonly used mocking library in Rust is `mockito`.

```rust
#[cfg(test)] mod tests {

use super::*;

use mockito::{mock, Matcher};

#[test]

fn test_api_request() {

let _m = mock("GET", "/resource")

.with_status(200)

.with_body("{\"key\": \"value\"}")

.create();

let response = reqwest::blocking::get(&format!("{}/resource", mockito::server_url())).unwrap();
assert_eq!(response.status(), 200);

let json_body: serde_json::Value = response.json().unwrap(); assert_eq!(json_body["key"], "value");

}

}
```

In this example, `mockito` allows for the creation of a mock server that responds to requests as if it were a real service. This approach makes your tests reliable, fast, and isolated.

By structuring your tests thoughtfully and leveraging tools like mocking libraries, you can gain confidence that your networking code will function as expected in real-world conditions. Remember to always keep your tests updated as your application evolves, ensuring comprehensive coverage across all functionalities.

Debugging Common Issues in Network Programming

However, as with any programming language, developers often face issues, especially when debugging network applications. This chapter explores common debugging strategies and techniques for tackling issues in network programming with Rust.

Understanding the Basics of Network Programming in Rust

Before delving into debugging, it's essential to have a basic understanding of how network programming works in Rust. Rust provides various libraries, notably the `std::net` module, which offers essential networking types and functions. Key components include TCP and UDP sockets for communication, the

`TcpStream` and `TcpListener` for handling connections, and asynchronous frameworks like `tokio` and

`async-std` for non-blocking I/O.

Common Issues in Network Programming

Network programming can introduce a plethora of issues

ranging from protocol mismatches to resource exhaustion. Understanding these issues will help in diagnosing and resolving them efficiently.

Connection Refusals: Attempting to connect to a server that isn't running or listening on the specified port.

Timeouts: Either client or server waiting too long for a response.

Data Corruption: Improper handling or encoding/decoding of data being sent and received.

Resource Leaks: Failing to properly close sockets can lead to resource exhaustion over time.

Concurrency Issues: Data races can occur when multiple threads or asynchronous tasks operate on shared data without proper synchronization.

Debugging Strategies ### 1. Logging

One of the simplest yet most effective ways to trace issues is by incorporating logging into your application. Rust's `log` crate provides a standardized way to log messages at various levels (error, warn, info, debug, trace).

```rust
use log::{info, error};

fn example_fn() {

info!("Starting connection process");

// ... connection logic

if let Err(e) = connect_to_server() { error!("Failed to connect: {}", e);

}
```

```
}
```

The key to effective logging is to provide enough context for each log entry. Instead of logging just an error message, include information such as the current operation, any relevant state, and timestamps.

2. Unit Testing and Integration Testing

Rust's built-in test framework allows developers to write tests for their functions easily. For network applications, it's crucial to write both unit tests and integration tests to ensure individual components work correctly together.

Unit tests can mock parts of the network stack, while integration tests can spin up real servers and clients. The `tokio` library also provides utilities to test asynchronous code effectively.

```rust
#[cfg(test)] mod tests {

use super::*;

#[test]

fn                        test_connection()                        {
assert!(connect_to_server().is_ok());

}

}
```

3. Network Analysis Tools

Using external tools can be beneficial to diagnose issues.

Wireshark, for example, is a network protocol analyzer that can capture and inspect network packets, helping you to see if messages are being sent correctly and if responses are valid.

4. Timeouts and Retries

Implementing timeouts for your network operations is a good safety measure. The `std::time::Duration` type can help define how long to wait before timing out. Coupled with retries, this can help overcome transient network issues.

```rust
use std::time::Duration;

let result = retry_with_timeout(|| connect_to_server(),
Duration::from_secs(5), 3);
```

5. Asynchronous Debugging

When using asynchronous programming (e.g., with `tokio`), debugging can become more complexed due to the non-linear flow of execution. Tools like `tokio-console` provide insights into asynchronous tasks, helping you visualize their state and the execution flow.

6. Handling Panic

Rust's panic mechanism can help catch critical errors. Properly handling panics in your network application can prevent unexpected crashes. Use `Result` and `Option` types to handle errors gracefully.

```rust
fn handle_request(req: Request) -> Result<Response,
```

```
Error> { if let Err(e) = process_request(req) {
return Err(Error::from(e)); // Handle error


}
Ok(Response::new())
}
```
```

By integrating these techniques into your workflow, you can greatly improve your ability to diagnose and resolve common networking issues, leading to more resilient and efficient applications. As with any programming endeavor, patience and persistence are key to mastering the complexities of network programming in Rust.
```

Conclusion

In this Book, we embarked on an exciting journey through the world of network programming with Rust, a language renowned for its performance, safety, and concurrency. We explored fundamental concepts, advanced techniques, and practical applications that enable you to build robust, fast, and secure networked systems.

Throughout our exploration, we witnessed the inherent advantages that Rust brings to network programming, particularly its focus on memory safety and zero-cost abstractions. We learned how Rust's type system and ownership model help prevent common pitfalls such as data races and memory leaks, allowing developers to focus on crafting high-quality, efficient applications.

We discussed essential libraries and frameworks like `Tokio` and `async-std`, which empower developers with the tools needed for asynchronous programming. This has become increasingly important in developin? responsive network applications that can handle multiple connections concurrently without compromising performance.

As we delved into various practical examples, we saw how to implement protocols, handle errors gracefully, and optimize our systems for both speed and reliability. We emphasized the importance of testing, debugging, and proactive performance profiling as integral aspects of the development lifecycle.

In conclusion, Rust represents a powerful option for those looking to excel in network programming. Its unique features enable developers to write code that is not only efficient but also secure, paving the way for the next generation of scalable applications. As you move forward in your journey with Rust, continue to experiment, learn, and innovate. Your contributions can lead to the development of systems that meet the demanding needs of modern networking while embracing the principles of safety and performance.

Thank you for joining me in this exploration of Rust for network programming. I hope the knowledge and insights shared throughout this eBook empower you to create impactful and transformative networked applications. Happy coding!

Biography

Jeff Stuart is a visionary writer and seasoned web developer with a passion for crafting dynamic and user-centric web applications. With years of hands-on experience in the tech industry, Jeff has mastered the art of problem-solving through code, specializing in Rust programming and cutting-edge web technologies. His expertise lies in creating efficient, scalable, and secure solutions that push the boundaries of what web applications can achieve.

As a lifelong learner and tech enthusiast, Jeff thrives on exploring the ever-evolving landscape of programming languages and frameworks. When he's not immersed in writing code or brainstorming innovative ideas, you'll find him sharing his knowledge through inspiring content that empowers others to unlock their full potential in the digital world.

Beyond his professional pursuits, Jeff enjoys exploring the

art of minimalist design, reading thought-provoking books on technology and philosophy, and hiking to recharge his creative energies. His unwavering dedication to excellence and his belief in the transformative power of technology shine through in every page of his work, making this book a compelling guide for anyone eager to master the art of Rust programming and web development.

Glossary: Rust for Network Programming

A

Asynchronous Programming: A programming paradigm that allows concurrent execution of tasks without blocking the main execution thread. In Rust, asynchronous programming is facilitated by the use of

`async`/`await` syntax.

Actor Model: A conceptual model used for building concurrent systems in which "actors" are the fundamental units of computation, encapsulating state and behavior. Rust's actors framework facilitates simplifying network interactions.

B

Blocking I/O: An I/O operation that causes the executing thread to wait until the operation completes. In network programming, blocking I/O can hinder performance and responsiveness.

Burnout: A term denoting the state of overwhelming stress and fatigue faced by developers, often caused by complex programming tasks or tight deadlines. Proper workload management is essential to avoid burnout, especially in networking projects that may require extensive debugging.

C

Crate: A package or library in Rust. Crates can be published to crates.io for others to use. In network programming, crates like `tokio` or `actix` provide useful abstractions for building networked applications.

Concurrency: The ability of a program to manage multiple tasks at the same time. Rust's ownership and borrowing model allows for safe concurrency, making it a compelling choice for network applications.

Client: A program or system that initiates a connection to a server and requests services. In network programming, a client could be a web browser, an API consumer, or any other client-side application.

D

Datagram: A self-contained, independent packet of data transmitted over a network. Used in connectionless protocols like UDP (User Datagram Protocol).

Dependency: A crate or module that another crate relies on in order to function. Managing dependencies is vital in Rust, where `Cargo` handles versioning and updates.

E

Error Handling: The process of managing errors that may occur during program execution. Rust emphasizes safety and provides robust mechanisms such as the

`Result` and `Option` types to handle errors without crashing the program.

Event Loop: A programming construct that waits for and dispatches events or messages in a program. In Rust's asynchronous programming model, the event loop is crucial for managing tasks without blocking.

G

Goroutine: Not directly related to Rust, but relevant in the context of concurrency. A goroutine is a lightweight thread in the Go programming language. Rust's model is more explicit, allowing for fine-grained control over concurrency without the overhead of goroutines.

H

HTTP (Hypertext Transfer Protocol): A protocol used for transmitting hypertext over the internet. Rust offers libraries like `hyper` for building efficient HTTP servers and clients.

Host: The machine or server providing a network service. In network programming, understanding the host environment is essential for proper implementation.

I

IP Address: A unique identifier for a device on a network, allowing it to communicate with other devices. IPv4 and IPv6 are the two versions most commonly used today.

I/O (Input/Output): Refers to the processes of receiving data from or sending data to an external source. In network programming, efficient I/O handling is critical for performance.

L

Library: A collection of pre-written code that developers can use to optimize their own coding efforts. In Rust, libraries can be included through crates, allowing for reusable components in network applications.

N

Network Socket: An endpoint of a two-way communication link between two programs running on the network. In Rust, `std::net` module provides necessary types for socket programming.

Non-blocking I/O: An I/O model that allows a program to continue execution while waiting for I/O operations to complete. Rust's `tokio` runtime provides tools for non-blocking network programming.

P

Protocol: A set of rules that define how data is formatted and processed in a network. Protocols like HTTP, TCP, and UDP govern how communication occurs between devices.

Packet: A formatted unit of data carried by a packet-switched network. Understanding packets is fundamental to network programming.

R

Runtime: The environment in which a program is executed. Rust's asynchronous runtimes, such as

`tokio` and `async-std`, facilitate efficient network operations.

Router: A networking device that forwards data packets between computer networks. In network programming, understanding routing is vital for creating effective client-server models.

S

Server: A program or system that provides services to clients over a network. In Rust, developers can build server applications using libraries like `actix-web` or `warp`.

Socket Programming: A form of network communication that involves the use of sockets to enable connection-oriented or connectionless communication between devices.

T

TCP (Transmission Control Protocol): A connection-oriented protocol that ensures reliable data transmission. It provides guarantees that data packets are delivered in the correct order and without error.

Thread: The smallest sequence of programmed instructions that can be managed independently by a scheduler. Rust's concurrency model provides a thread-safe way of handling multiple concurrent operations.

U

UDP (User Datagram Protocol): A connectionless protocol that allows for quicker transmissions at the cost of reliability. It is often used in applications where speed is critical and some data loss is acceptable.

URI (Uniform Resource Identifier): A string that identifies a particular resource. URIs are often used in web applications to access resources over the internet.

W

WebSocket: A protocol for full-duplex communication channels over a single TCP connection. Rust has libraries like `tokio-tungstenite` for easily implementing WebSocket servers and clients.